God**ENCOUNTERS**

PURSUING A 24/7 EXPERIENCE
OF JESUS

*God*ENCOUNTERS

PURSUING A 24/7 EXPERIENCE OF JESUS

BY A. ALLAN MARTIN, SHAYNA BAILEY & LYNELL LAMOUNTAIN

Pacific Press® Publishing Association
Nampa, Idaho
Oshawa, Ontario, Canada
www.pacificpress.com

Cover design by David Leach
Inside design by Aaron Troia

Copyright © 2009 by Pacific Press® Publishing Association
Printed in the United States of America
All rights reserved

You can obtain additional copies of this book by calling toll-free 1-800-765-6955 or by visiting http://www.adventistbookcenter.com.

ISBN 13: 978-0-8163-2339-5
ISBN 10: 0-8163-2339-9

09 10 11 12 13 • 5 4 3 2 1

CONTENTS

Dedication

from Lynell—

To Jennifer for believing in me 24/7 and for your love and companionship through it all.

To Garrison, you are the joy of my life—you've truly shown me what GOD is like through your unconditional love.

To Mom and Dad, and my whole family, for sharing the grace of Christ and His eternal hope. I love you all more than you can know.

To you, fellow GODseeker, for the joy of taking this unforgettable journey with you. Many, many blessings.

from Shayna—

To my mother, Anesta Thomas, for instilling a love for GOD and His word in my heart.

To my sister, Niesha, for always reminding me that my writing was worth reading.

To the GODencounters generation, for daring to go deeper, think harder, and live differently.

from Allan—

Deirdre, your faithfulness to JC inspires my life...

Alexa, your love for Jesus impresses my heart...

Mama & Papa, your loyalty to GOD forms my courage...

I cherish you all as fellow GODfollowers on the journey.

1.0 GODENCOUNTERS:
A PREFACE

1.1 Sacred Discontent

(A. Allan Martin)

I'm just sick of it. Aren't you?

If you find yourself dissatisfied with just going to church, then this book is for you.

If you feel it is not enough to know *about* GOD, you are in good company.

If you long for something beyond superficial, shallow relationships, then you're in the same boat as me.

When you can't keep living the way you've been living; when you feel a sense of being lost just going through the motions (even though you are seemingly a "pretty good person"); when you want something more than religion, that's what I call *sacred discontent.*

At the the turn of the century, I began a journey called GODencounters that changed my life. I have gotten a taste of being in GOD's presence; it has transformed me. And along the way, this new experience has changed my sense of community as well.

In the coming entries, you will hear and sense many voices. These are voices of young adults whose lives have intersected in unexpected ways because of GODencounters. Maybe they came for a variety of reasons, but once they encountered the living GOD, everything changed.

GODencounters has revealed a different life from the one I was living. I have found myself wanting more . . . more of GOD. More of who He is . . . simply something more. In this book, you will cross paths with others just as discontented as you—others who hunger for something deep and real. Although the entries may seem eclectic, at times disjointed, I encourage you to listen intently for the common strands in the entries. There are stories within the stories, and themes that carry through. Find a GODstory in the tapestry of experiences.

A vital portion of this book is the encounter questions. Take your time in responding. Give these inquiries some devoted attention, allowing your story to weave new strands into GODencounters. Your story is priceless, an important thread to add to the collection of experiences found in these pages.

It is my prayer that as you move through the entries, you will sense your own sacred discontent. I'm trusting GOD to give you a taste of His goodness and leave you wanting ever more of Him.

1.2 What is GODencounters?

(A. Allan Martin)

GODencounters is a movement of young adults who are wholeheartedly seeking a 24/7 experience of GOD, recklessly living for His renown. Daring to deepen intimacy with GOD, the GODencounters experience gives focus to seven discipleship themes in which practices of the Christian faith are emphasized. "We prayed GODencounters would be a catalyst for deep, personal experiences with GOD," cofounder Jeff Gang says. "[GODencounters is] not an act or a program, but an everyday, every-moment way of living." GODencounters aims to deepen devotion to Jesus by developing disciples, walking recklessly in His footsteps.

Our desire is to

+ live lives of **Worship;**
+ be agents of the **Gospel;**
+ **Grace**-fully express compassion;
+ **Pray** without ceasing;
+ embrace **Sabbath** as soul CPR;
+ **Morph** into His likeness;
+ and celebrate in **Jubilee.**

Through holy gatherings and private worship, GODencounters disciples are living out these seven precepts of discipleship. In cyberspace, in real time, and through these devos, young adults are returning to the heart of GOD, growing a movement of GODfollowers pursuing GODencountered lives, 24/7.

"I have felt far from GOD for a while now, and in need of spiritual renewal and counsel," shares humanities and environmental studies major Stephanie Cato. "I embraced the practical advice of GODencounters and, through the Holy Spirit, have put my feet and eyes back on the path."

Return to the heart of GOD.

Encounter the Word

"I will give them a heart to know me, that I am the LORD. They will be my people, and I will be their God, for they will return to me with all their heart" (Jeremiah 24:7, NIV).

Encounter

+ How close or far do you feel from GOD? What kind of life do you wish to have with Him? Why?
+ What type of crowd do you feel most comfortable being with? What type of people do you feel GOD cares the most about?
+ Take a moment. What type of GODencounter do you desire? What would it be like for you to be in His presence?

1.3 In the Presence of GOD and Each Other

(Erika Larson-Hueneke)

When I walked into GODencounters conference the first time, I was church-less. I had been living in Florida for eight months, and I had no church to call my home. It wasn't that I hadn't tried. I had been to Baptist churches, charismatic churches, and nondenominational churches. I didn't care much about the label; I just wanted Jesus, and I wanted to find some friends who wanted Him too. But I wandered around, never feeling quite like I fit in, never feeling truly challenged to make the uncomfortable changes, to initiate the difficult conversations.

And then I met a boy. We had been dating for about two weeks when he took me to GODencounters conference (GEc)—a gathering of young adults hungry to experience GOD, whether through listening to a speaker, participating in musical worship, spending time in a prayer room, or conversing with a fellow GODseeker.

After my first GEc, I stood in the candlelit café, a little nervous, a little self-conscious. But before long, I realized I was among friends, and we found ourselves talking about the "church," with all its traditions and nuances, some of them weird, some of them wonderful, some both.

Two years later when I walked into GODencounters conference, I greeted some friends from that first year, as well as some new friends from the local faith community I finally found, that I finally committed to. I wasn't nervous at all, just excited for all of us to be together. But a funny thing happens when you decide to join a faith community—when you choose to pursue these people and know them deeply, their beauty and their brokenness—you end up meeting *GOD* on a deeper level.

I guess that's the whole point of GODencounters and life in general—meeting deeply with GOD, and meeting deeply with people.

The most recent conference's emphasis was prayer, which we tend to think of as something that happens between one person and GOD. But the people I spoke with at GEc told me something interesting—they told me the moments of prayer they most remembered were times when they came to GOD *with someone else.* They said the worships that made them feel most alive were the times they lifted their voices and hands *beside their friends.* They shared that they often found the most encouragement in helping *another person* to experience a personal encounter with GOD.

The results of such discoveries, I found, were beautifully varied. Elia King, the conference's worship leader, shared that GEc helped him realize that he often takes the GODencounters around him for granted. "I was just really challenged to think about my relationships with other people and how often I take people for granted," he told me. "Every year I come, my thinking about my relationship with GOD and my relationships with other people has been challenged."

Lyris Bacchus, who coordinated volunteers for GEc, shared this: "I've had a chance to pray with people personally, and to me, that's been a GODencounter in and of itself, in GOD leading that person to me, knowing that I could be part of helping them to find GOD's answer . . . That's just so humbling to me. I feel so privileged to be able to do that." Lyris and the other volunteers who work behind the scenes at GEc seek to stretch young adults to experience GOD in ways that might at first feel uncomfortable, but will hopefully bring blessing and deeper intimacy with Jesus.

Prayer room coordinator Heather Magray believes that introducing people to corporate contemplative practices such as *lectio divina* and centering prayer, and also to experimental prayer rooms like the ones set up to allow visitors to pray through the different stations of the Cross and of the Old Testament sanctuary, helps to stretch them out of their comfort zones. "GOD wants to stretch us," she said. "I think it's helping us to look at things a little bit different and more open-mindedly, and that can be hard—it's hard for me to do that. But we're giving people permission to do that."

The climax of the prayer experience at GEc was the Boiler Room, a prayer room that stayed open for twenty-four hours straight, through all the watches of the night. The individuals who faithfully kept up the continuous prayer did so privately and in groups; quietly and loudly; mournfully and joyfully; written, spoken, sung, or drawn.

My personal experience in the Boiler Room began at 8:00 A.M. When my fiancé (the same boy who first brought me to GEc two years earlier) and I arrived, two men were silently praying individually, candles were burning, and music was playing softly. I took a spot on a large cushion on the floor and began to write out my jumbled thoughts—confessions of prideful attitudes, fears, laziness, and distorted priorities. It was a very personal time of reconnecting with GOD, whom I had been mostly ignoring for weeks. When I had finished pouring out my heart, I felt free to turn up the celebratory music and dance before GOD, and my time closed with my fiancé and I taking Communion together. I was surprised that I easily spent two hours there.

Others shared Boiler Room stories with me of finding healing and freedom from destructive thoughts of the past; of attending an anointing workshop and then almost immediately having the chance to anoint someone in the prayer room; of praying for GOD's Spirit to be present at GEc and then watching a sanctuary full of people come to life in worship. The heart cries uttered in the prayer rooms without a doubt translated into the heartfelt worship sessions of GODencounters.

Allan Martin, the curriculum coach for GODencounters, shared with me his experience of the last session: "We had Communion, which isn't uncommon, but there was this weird thing that happened. Everything was done, but you could palpably feel that everyone wanted to linger. They didn't want to go. And to me, it was like, I've been to so many of these events—people usually just dash out because they have something else to do. But when GODencounters came to its last night and we had remembered GOD through Communion, the conference was over. There was no more café. There was nothing left. Yet all of us remained there with Him—lingering—because we sensed GOD's presence and we didn't want to leave."

Being in the presence of GOD and each other is the heart of GODencounters, and the hope of those involved behind the scenes is that this connection, this deep togetherness, will continue on, and that prayer will truly become a ceaseless conversation with Christ. "The core of GODencounters," Allan said, "is what we've called a *sacred discontent*—that we experience the holy, living GOD, and come away unable to be satisfied with what was 'good enough' before."

I know.

I and my community of fellow GODseekers certainly left with a deepened desire for more.

Encounter the Word

" 'For I know the plans I have for you,' " declares the Lord, 'plans to prosper you and not to harm you, plans to give you hope and a future. Then you will call upon me and come and pray to me, and I will listen to you. You will seek me and find me when you seek me with all your heart' " (Jeremiah 29:11–13, NIV).

Encounter

+ What has been on your mind lately that you haven't shared with anyone? Who do you feel is safe to share your thoughts with?
+ What do you believe is GOD's intent for you? What's keeping you from embracing His plan?
+ What are you seeking after?

1.4 The Desires of My Heart

(A. Allan Martin)

It's been a year now, adjusting to a new place, a new job, and a new challenge. One of the realities that struck me hard is returning to the role of "church shopper," having been displaced by GOD from our previous spiritual home.

It doesn't help that there are dozens of choices. It's so overwhelming and disheartening.

So here we are "kickin' the tires" and taking "test drives," to see if GOD has a church in mind for us. More than ever before, I long for GODencounters and the community it affords. I am envious to the point of sin of the GODencounters conferences and retreats common to the state where I lived before, knowing constantly the embrace of GODfollowing friends and colleagues. The saturating awe of being in GOD's presence with a holy recklessness is hard to live without.

I miss being with Deeper or SomethingMORE or Celebration Seventh-day Adventist Church, the congregations where the sense of community was real and had become more intimate for me over the years. I had settled my family into a place and found faith communities that felt like home. It was all so cozy—great friends, warm congregations, and familiar routines. Then GOD moved us to another place, with the not-so-cozy task of starting over.

But as I enjoy the return of Sabbath with the setting of the afternoon sun after a busy Friday afternoon, my mind turns to a passage that has become my GODencounters mantra: " 'I will give them the desire to know that I am the Lord. Then they will be my people, and I will be their God, because they will return to me with all their heart' " (Jeremiah 24:7, GNT). It rings true in my soul. I desire knowledge of GOD. I seek GOD's presence. I covet belonging to GOD. I come to Him with all my heart.

Although I have been "displaced" from communities/churches that had been a spiritual haven for me, I still have GOD. And maybe GOD wants the GODencounters in my life to be focused on Him and not on people, places, or things. Maybe He wants me to return to Him with all my heart.

Sure, I have no doubt He will bless with a thriving, authentic place to fellowship with other GODfollowers. But if the mantra is sinking into my soul, I think He is calling me into fellowship with Him. Maybe the point is GOD.

"O GOD, be the desire of my heart. Inject into my bloodstream Your desire. Reveal my identity in You. Return me to the heart of worship. Return me to You, with all my heart."

Encounter the Word

Read Hebrews 11, and then give special attention and meditation to the following verse:

"All these people were still living by faith when they died. They did not receive the things promised; they only saw them and welcomed them from a distance. And they admitted that they were aliens and strangers on earth" (Hebrews 11:13, NIV).

Encounter

+ In what ways is your life comfortable right now? How does that sense of ease affect your spiritual journey?
+ When do you cling tightest to GOD? Why?
+ How can challenges in your life benefit your relationship with GOD? And your relationship with others?
+ What would "living by faith" look like for you? Elaborate and take notes on this thought.

My Experience

_____

_____

_____

_____

_____

_____

_____

_____

2.0 WORSHIP

2.1 Live Lives of Worship

It is our desire to experience the presence of the living GOD 24/7. Beyond religious rituals expressed occasionally, we're learning to worship GOD as a way of living life.

2.2 The Secret

(Jeff Gang)

> Fwd: >Fwd: >FWD: >Fwd: The Secret Is Out! (you gotta read this!)!?!

Is it everybody, or am I the only one who doesn't like e-mail forwards? It's annoying. Listen, people. I don't read them. I can't find the Delete key fast enough. Please stop sending them to me.

However, I've come to realize that there's one forward in life I can't ignore—I can't delete it because it won't go away. It has been sent down through the ages. It's been passed on from generation to generation, from century to century, from decade to decade. Through the millennia it comes down. The message is clear. It reads as follows:

<< In a message dated "before the dawn of time"
>00:00:00 from somewhere in the universe,
>[e-mail address] writes:
>

><<
>THE SECRET IS OUT This was written by the Creator
>The kingdom of heavens . . .
>
>Listen!
>I am the revealer of secrets.
>I am the revealer of great mysteries from before time immortal.
>I know great things!
>
>
>I can't keep it inside; I can't keep this secret. It's
>too amazing.
>It's too incredible. It's too wonderful! I
>am bursting to tell you. I will die to tell you.
>
>
>Here it is: Are you ready?
>I am the One who formed your inward parts;
> I knit you together in your mother's womb.
>You are wonderfully made.
>
>My ways are not hidden from you,
>you were made in secret,
>intricately woven in the depths of the earth.
>But my eyes beheld your unformed substance.
>
>And listen! In my book were written
>all the days that were formed for you,
>when none of them as yet existed.
>
>I know these thoughts blow your mind. I know
>how boggling this secret is to your thoughts,
>how vast is the sum total of what I am revealing!

>
>Try to count them—but you can't—they are more
>than the sand; you'll come to the end of every grain
>—I am still with you!
>
>
>I am GOD.
>
>
>Now if you are amazed by this Revealer of Secrets,
>forward this to all the people in your address book
>and the person who sent
>this to you.
> >>

Encounter Prayer

"O Revealer of Secrets, I worship You today and every day. You are Bigger than me. You are Greater than my sum total. I bow before You in awe and wonder. I come before You with praise. You who revealed my destiny before I was. Because You Were and You Are. Amen."

Encounter the Word

"As you were lying there, O king, your mind turned to things to come, and the revealer of mysteries showed you what is going to happen" (Daniel 2:29, NIV).

Encounter

+ The secret is out. What difference is it going to make in your life today?
+ What perceptions have changed for you? What can no longer be the same with what you now know?
+ What difference will this secret make in your life the next time you worship (alone or with people)?
+ Why is this secret so important to living a life of GODencounters?

2.3 He Could, so He Did

(Lynell LaMountain)

I took a giant stride off the back of the dive boat and plunged into the bluest, clearest water I'd seen in three years. Purging the air from my vest, I glided forty-five feet to the sandy bottom that was decorated by brain coral outcroppings and schools of blue tang, trumpet fish, and queen angels. The water temperature was 83 degrees. I could see sixty-five feet in every direction. And all I could think was, *Wow . . . my Father created this.*

Our ever-smiling dive master, Bero, a jolly, Swedelike man with long white hair (imagine Santa Clause without a beard but with a thick Danish accent) led our drift dive. A few minutes into it, he finned over to hand me something. Into my cupped hands he delicately placed a baby spider starfish. It was brown, about five inches across, and had fuzzy, spaghettilike legs. It danced and tickled my fingers; then I handed it to my wife, Jennifer, for her to enjoy. When I turned around, Bero was floating on his back, holding his regulator in one hand and blowing "smoke rings" toward the surface, which spiraled upward like wobbly disks of Jell-O. A little later, near the end of our dive, an octopus played hide-and-go-seek with us, collapsing its spongy body and darting into a hole inside the coral.

After forty-five minutes, it was time for us to surface. I didn't want the dive to end. I looked around, taking mental snapshots of this oceanic paradise, hoping to remember always what it looked like.

The thought had occurred to me during the dive that GOD didn't have to create the ocean with such colorful, iridescent beauty. Most of the time, we don't see what's under the water anyway. Few people ever learn the skills required to venture into this enchanting world. Think about it: not only did GOD create the heavens and the earth, but He also populated them with stars and planets and moons and eagles and pelicans and dolphins and whales and spider starfish.

I'm not sure what that means to you, but to me it means that our GOD enjoys beauty for beauty's sake. An uncaring, utilitarian god would have clothed the world in gray, with vast, empty spaces, considering all that other stuff "unnecessary."

And it is . . . unless you're a Creator who loves variety and colors and life and smiles and the unnecessary.

There's something else GOD did: He created somebody to share it with—

you. "God said, 'Let Us make man in Our image, according to Our likeness; and let them rule over the fish of the sea and over the birds of the sky and' . . . God created man in His own image . . . God saw all that He had made, and behold, it was very good" (Genesis 1:26, 27, 31, NASB). Everything GOD made was very good—including you.

Encounter

- ◆ What experiences have you had that inspired awe in you?
- ◆ What would you identify as the top five most beautiful things you have ever seen in person?
- ◆ Who do you enjoy sharing beautiful things with? What motivates you to bring it to their attention?
- ◆ What might you imagine was GOD's intention in creating beauty?

2.35 Will Yourself

(Lynell LaMountain)

If you read **2.3**, then you know that Jennifer and I took a spectacular scuba dive off the coast of Aruba.[1] What you probably don't know is this: I'm afraid of the water.

I've never been comfortable in the water. I'm the kid you always saw gripping the side of the pool. Nothing short of an act of GOD could have pried my white-knuckled fingers from the edge. As long as I was grasping the edge, I was safe and would survive another day . . . only to jump into the pool and cling to the side in terror once again.

So here I am now, diving 45, 60, 90, 110 feet (I know!) and thinking, *Acres and acres of ocean above my head—and I'm still alive! I'm not dying! Wow! This is too cool! Wait a second! Is that a shark I see over there? Nope. Just my shadow reflecting against the coral.*

Something has started happening recently to this fear-managing, curiosity-driven scuba diver: I've started to enjoy diving. Can you believe it? I've logged enough dives to know that I can rely on my tank, gauges, vest, and regulators. I can relax and enjoy my dives because, through experience, I've learned that my

---

1. The dive site is called Dantchi's Delight, and it's only eight minutes off the coast of Aruba.

equipment is trustworthy. In the unlikely event that something should go wrong, I have my trustworthy dive buddy (Jennifer) and her trustworthy equipment, and our trustworthy dive master, who's logged ten-thousand plus dives (and life insurance).

From the edge of the pool to the bottom of the ocean—what a leap!

I'm not sure if you would agree, but I don't think you can really enjoy life scuttling along the edge of the pool. At some point, you've got to dive in and do the thing you're afraid of! If you have to will yourself, then will yourself.

Do it!

Get yourself out on the floor and tango with life—dance with GOD into the arms of Eternity (He won't drop you; you can trust Him).

Believe me, it was with a pounding heart that I willed myself for the first time to jump off the back of a dive boat a few years ago, to descend seventy feet onto a ghostly barge at the bottom of the sea, and into a squadron of bubble-eyed stingrays that purposely buzzed my head like Maverick buzzing the tower with his F-16 in *Top Gun*. I was nervous and so anxious *not* to die that I drained my tank in ten minutes (whereas on Monday, when the dive ended after forty-five minutes, I still had thirty minutes of air left).

Man, I'm so glad I let go and took that first leap several years ago. If I had not, my life would've been a partially finished masterpiece (in some ways, it still is).

Scientists tell us that we're born with only two legitimate fears: the fear of falling and the fear of loud noises. All our other fears are learned. That's wonderful news! Why? Because anything that's been learned can be what? Unlearned![2]

Don't let imaginary spooks scare you into a dark, lonely corner. Your purpose in life is to live and be happy. Isn't it time you took the leap?

Encounter the Word

"Trust in the LORD with all your heart and lean not on your own understanding; in all your ways acknowledge him, and he will make your paths straight" (Proverbs 3:5, 6, NIV).

---

2. Now, my trustworthy dive buddy (Jennifer, a.k.a. loving wife) wants me to go sky diving with her. May I politely refer you (and her) to legitimate fear #1?

Encounter

+ What fears have you learned? Where has your trust been broken? What is preventing you from experiencing life to the full?

+ How might you rebuild your trust in GOD's faithfulness? What are the first steps you will take?

+ Where in your life can you acknowledge that GOD has been asking you to "leap"? What adventures might you imagine He has in store for you?

2.4 LORD, Help Me Be Afraid

(Elisa Brown)

When Jesus was on this earth, He told His followers multiple times not to be afraid. It seems as though every time He revealed Himself in a new way, He had to tell them not to fear (look at Matthew 8:26; 17:7; Mark 4:40; Luke 5:10; John 6:20). Whatever had just happened left them shaking with fear, and only after He reassured them did they begin to internalize the deeper meaning of what was revealed.

Recently, I listened to a radio show by Christian musician Michael Card, and he was discussing the fact of the disciples' fear. I was challenged by Michael's question: "When was the last time we were afraid of GOD?"[3]

Immediately you are thinking this is a ridiculous question, since we have been taught our whole lives that there is no reason to be afraid of GOD. In 1741, Jonathan Edwards preached a sermon entitled, "Sinners in the Hands of an Angry God." In it he portrays GOD as the "God that holds you over the pit of hell, much as one holds a spider, or some loathsome insect over the fire, abhors you, and is dreadfully provoked: his wrath towards you burns like fire; he looks upon you as worthy of nothing else, but to be cast into the fire."[4] It seems that ever since that era of teaching, many well-meaning Christians have been working to quell the myth of a GOD whose punishment we must fear and who has nothing but anger and hatred for us.

---

3. http://www.michaelcard.com.

4. Jonathan Edwards, *Sermons and Discourses, 1739-1742 (WJE Online Vol. 22)*, Ed. Harry S. Stout, 410. Retrieved from the Jonathan Edwards Center at Yale University, http://edwards.yale.edu/archive?path= aHR0cDovL2Vkd2FyZHMueWFsZS5lZHUvY2dpLWJpbi9uZXdwaGlsby9ZZXRvbplY3QucGGw/ Yy4yMTo0Ny53amVv (accessed on December 5, 2008).

Upon reflecting, though, I wonder if we have gone so far in trying to help people understand the love of GOD that we have forgotten to have fear. We no longer tremble in His presence or take our shoes off when we are on holy ground. We have lost sight of His power, and nothing strikes awe in us anymore, let alone fear.

One of the ways the *Merriam-Webster* dictionary defines *fear* is "profound reverence and awe especially toward God."[5] What would it take to make you tremble in awe and reverence before the GOD who holds the worlds in His hands? If He is the same yesterday, today, and tomorrow, why do we not feel astonished and afraid when GOD reveals Himself?

Encounter the Word

"And now, O Israel, what does the LORD your God ask of you but to fear the LORD your God, to walk in all his ways, to love him, to serve the LORD your God with all your heart and with all your soul, and to observe the LORD's commands and decrees that I am giving you today for your own good?" (Deuteronomy 10:12, 13, NIV).

Encounter

+ Listen to the words of the song "Tremble" by Nicole Nordeman.[6] Reflect and consider what part of your life forgets to tremble.
+ When was the last time you were afraid of GOD? What caused your fear?
+ What strikes "profound reverence or awe" in you? Explain.
+ How would you define the difference between the "fear" the disciples experienced and the "fear" being advocated in Deuteronomy 10?
+ In what ways can "fearing" and "loving" GOD happen simultaneously? Can you love GOD and yet fear Him? Explain.

---

5. *Merriam-Webster Online*, s.v. "fear [noun]," http://www.merriam-webster.com/dictionary/fear%5B2%5D (accessed December 5, 2008).

6. To read the lyrics, go to http://www.top50lyrics.com/n/nicolenordeman-lyrics-20851/tremble-lyrics-548663.html or do an online search for "Nicole Nordeman Tremble."

2.5 Invisible

(Tim Goff)

"Now faith is being sure of what we hope for and certain of what we do not see" (Hebrews 11:1, NIV). Yes, LORD, I am reading this but . . . that is s-o-o-o not like me. I want to see, hear, and then believe! I want to see Your glory and see Your face and see the way You smile with grace. I want to hear Your voice, catch the tone and inflection of what You are saying, and draw from this my trust. But You have chosen to make Yourself invisible.

Jesus, You spoke about the importance of having eyes to see and ears to hear. Well, do You want me to see You and hear Your voice? I am waiting . . . LORD, You want me to follow You, but how can I follow if I cannot see and hear You? My senses are all I have to know what is going on around me. So what shall it be, LORD? What good are eyes and ears if I cannot see and hear You?

Yet You healed the blind and gave them sight. Now I am really confused, LORD. I am beginning to understand that You must have a very different plan than what I expect. Open the eyes of my heart, LORD, and open the ears of my soul so that I may experience You. For nothing I have, neither my eyes, ears, touch, smell, nor taste, can do it for me. I can't get in touch or hear You with my abilities. Therefore, if I am to have fellowship with the Invisible, it must be true that You meet Your people by some other way. Is that what revelation is?

OK, I am starting to get it, LORD. I need to forget my expectations and abilities and open my heart to inspiration from You. So, LORD, since I cannot seek You through my senses, can I not seek You at all, much less find You? After all, how could I find You without my senses, if that is all I have? If so, then how does this happen?

Is it possible that my worship of You is not so much about me seeking You but is rather my response to what You are already putting in my heart? Wow, this is getting interesting (and heavy). If this is true, then my worship, prayers, songs, and devotions are a free response to a heart calling. You must have put it there in the first place, which means that since I cannot seek an invisible GOD, You are the One seeking me . . . and . . . and this means that all my spiritual strength and all my understanding of eternal things comes from You in the first place! *Whoa.*

Yes, LORD, then open the eyes of my heart and open the ears of my soul, so that I can sense Your presence and know You instead of all the images, sounds, smells, tastes, and feelings I have. O that my response could be a reflection without fingerprints or smudges of what You are allowing me to see in my heart about You. Thank You, LORD, for putting this love in my heart (and being invisible).

Encounter the Word

"Now to the King eternal, immortal, invisible, the only God, be honor and glory for ever and ever. Amen" (1 Timothy 1:17, NIV).

Encounter

+ What do you sense (beyond your senses)?
+ What has GOD already put in your heart and seeded in your life?
+ How have you sensed GOD's pursuit of you?

2.6 Let Less Be Less

(A. Allan Martin)

Gluttony. That's it, plain and simple. I am a voluntary victim of it. Saturated, steeped, and soaked in it. Every cultural pore in my being oozes it. I thought my generation had transcended the brash consumerism of those before us. I thought young adults were superior because we disown the extravagance of generations past. I scoffed at their bumper stickers proclaiming, "I'm spending my children's inheritance." "He who dies with the most toys wins," was a cultural motto that I condescendingly frowned on.

But now, becoming part of the next "thirty-something" generation, I find myself just as fat on the frivolous as those who walked here before. "More for me" still reigns, and it has me in its gobbling grip.

Cases in point . . .

I let the waiter think my nephew was three years old, so I could get his meal for free.

I complained and argued until I got my way with the bank, which begrudgingly refunded me an ATM fee. (My error or their error? It's still up for debate . . .

headed to the Supreme Court, I'm sure.)

I want more iTunes, more prestige, more rebounds, more respect, more vacation time, more books, and more speed on the Internet so-that-I-can-get-more-stuff-faster-and-for-less-than-it-would-cost-me-retail.

And through it all, I could say to you I am better than the gluttons of the past because I am striving for less, because . . . "Less is more."

How elegant, how retro, how responsible (how about getting past the baloney!). Even in that superficial statement, I am still trying to get more (recognition, sophistication, altruism points). More for me! MORE for ME! ME! ME! ME!

Gluttony. Plain and simple.

Funny how I am what I detest. So funny, it's unfunny.

Maybe it's time for a new thing.

"He must become greater; I must become less" (John 3:30, NIV). "He" is Jesus. "Jesus, let less be less. Let me dwindle down to a core . . . a core of contrite, needy dependence on You. Less of me; make it all about You."

Let less be less.

Encounter the Word

Read Philippians 2, and then give special attention and meditation to the following passage:

> Your attitude should be the same as that of Christ Jesus:
> Who, being in very nature God,
>   did not consider equality with God something to be grasped,
> but made himself nothing,
>   taking the very nature of a servant,
>   being made in human likeness.
> And being found in appearance as a man,
>   he humbled himself
>   and became obedient to death—
>   even death on a cross! (Philippians 2:5–8, NIV).

Encounter

+ What are you consuming the most? What consumes you?

- What impact would "less of you" have on your self-esteem?
- What would it mean to be more dependent?
- How is dependency on GOD different from dysfunctional dependency? Explain.
- What could lessen the grip of gluttony on you today?

2.7 View the Master

(Jeff Gang)

One of my favorite toys growing up was the View-Master. Maybe you remember this toy. It was a strange contraption that looked like demented binoculars. There was a slot in the top where you were supposed to put this cardboard wheel with mini-slides around it. Then you pulled down on the lever to advance the slides while peering through the lenses and you had your own private 3-D slide show—from cartoons and comic book heroes to tours of Africa. It was great!

We've all been given a View-Master. It's called the life and teachings of Jesus. He came to show us how to live the kingdom life. Nicodemus recognized Him as a Teacher sent from GOD. More important, Nicodemus recognized, as did many others, that what Jesus was teaching said a lot about how we are to relate to GOD and one another. The Gospels continually refer to people being "amazed" by what they witnessed in the life and teachings of this simple Man from a town called Nazareth.

Jesus is the ultimate View-Master. He shows us how to live a life of connections with GOD and people.

One of the key things He taught us was how to worship. Worship, for Jesus, didn't just happen at the synagogue on Sabbath. He lived a life of worship. It was His state of being. It meant that He related to His Father and His brothers and sisters differently than He would have otherwise. True worship does that to you. It changes your perspective. So make sure you View the Master today.

Encounter Prayer

"LORD Jesus, You are my Teacher. May I learn from You today. Help me to see things through Your eyes. Change my perspective. May I view Your life today and follow after Your ways and Your methods."

Encounter the Word

"He came to Jesus at night and said, 'Rabbi, we know you are a teacher who has come from God. For no one could perform the miraculous signs you are doing if God were not with him'" (John 3:2, NIV).

Encounter

+ What do you see when you View the Master?
+ What are some things Jesus did that may change your perspective on living a life of worship versus viewing worship as simply a once-a-week act?
+ If you were in Nicodemus's shoes, what questions would you have for Jesus?
+ What are the signs of Jesus in your life?

2.8 RSVP

(Annette Alfonso)

RSVP—*répondez s'il vous plait*. For those of us whose strength is not the French language, this means "please reply." How often do we get these RSVPs for weddings, baby showers, reunions, and whatever event for which the host would like to know who wishes to come? Who will accept the invitation?

How often do we intend to respond and somehow it gets shuffled in with the junk mail, only to be unearthed five months too late?

Every moment of our lives, we are given an RSVP from GOD.

He invites us to spend time with Him and wants to know if we will come. He wants to know if we will accept His invitation. Throughout Scripture, He invites us to draw near to Him and to seek Him. GOD is pleading, "My dear one, I want us to spend every moment together. Please accept My invitation to be with you."

But how can we accept an invitation for constant time with Him? We have deadlines to meet, successes to attain, feats to accomplish. How can we add one more thing to our already overbooked daily lists of things to do? After all, success is made; it is earned. We have to work for what we have if we want it at all. We worry about finances. We get stressed about relationships. We take medications to help curb our nerves. We obsess about the future and what it may hold.

In Jeremiah 29:11–13, GOD acknowledges those worries as He invites us. He who created our innermost being knows how easily we get stressed out. In my paraphrase of the passage, GOD says, "Chill out. I have it all under control. I have a wonderful future for you that, if you just trust Me, you will see it unfold in a marvelous way. Call for Me. Pray, and I AM listening.

"When you scramble to seek Me, I am found. You don't need to stress about your career or success, for I have all of your successes in My hands.

"I know what brings you greatest joy. I know what career you should choose. I know where you should live. I know whom you will marry, when you will have children. I know it all and want you to experience My plan for you.

"Now . . . will you trust Me? Will you believe that I have it all under control? Will you accept My invitation and spend time with Me? For the more time we spend together, the more you will understand how much I love you and how great is My plan for your life.

"I can't make you accept My invitation. It can just as easily get stashed away with the junk mail. It is your decision to accept or decline My invitation. RSVP Please reply . . ."

Encounter the Word

" 'For I know the plans I have for you,' declares the LORD, 'plans to prosper you and not to harm you, plans to give you hope and a future. Then you will call upon me and come and pray to me, and I will listen to you. You will seek me and find me when you seek me with all your heart' " (Jeremiah 29:11–13, NIV).

Encounter

+ What clutter in your life has covered over GOD's RSVP?
+ Today, what will be your reply?
+ How, specifically, will you accept GOD's invitation to spend time with Him?

2.9 Fight Back Like This

(Lynell LaMountain)

When was the last time someone talked about you behind your back?

When was the last time you were mocked, insulted, humiliated, or the target of malicious gossip?

The world is filled with abusers—people who abuse you emotionally, mentally, and spiritually. You have at least four options in dealing with them:

1. Stick your head in the sand and not deal with them.
2. Allow yourself to continue being abused by them.
3. Wallow in despair, self-pity, sadness, or addiction.
4. Find refuge in GOD from these spiritual molesters.

King David chose number four. I read Psalm 69 this morning, in which David talks about all the garbage he was taking from people. (If you want to feel better about your life, read about David's experience with abusers in Psalm 69!) David found refuge in GOD during his time of emotional and spiritual oppression. And He asked GOD to do some surprising things. He asked GOD to . . .

1. Save him.
2. Rescue him from these molesters.
3. Judge his oppressors accordingly.
4. Blot their names from the book of life (wow!).
5. And protect him during his time of pain and distress.

During his time of personal persecution by these godless people, when his vision was blurred with tears and his throat ached with sorrow, David found peace, deliverance, and divine vindication. He never stopped worshiping GOD either. "I will praise God's name in song and glorify him with thanksgiving," he wrote (Psalm 69:30, NIV).

GOD has adopted you into His family. Whatever people do to you, they are doing to Him. Period. You need to know this, believe this, and understand this.

You're not a doormat. You're not a punching bag. According to David, GOD's plan isn't for you to stand there and be miserable about yourself so that others can feel good about themselves.

But here's the key question: How do you fight back?

David says you fight back through worship and personal devotion to GOD.

What's worship? It's submission to GOD's sovereign will (look at Romans 12:1, 2).

When you're crying and hurting and lonely, go to GOD. Find rest in Him. Plead your case. Ask Him to save you, rescue you, protect you, and *vindicate* you. He will hear your cries. And He will answer your prayer.

I know this is a tough situation. It's even tougher when your tormentor is sitting across the church aisle with his or her Bible open and a "prayer" on his or her lips. So what? You know in your heart that it's just theater—they're only acting. (Remember this: it doesn't matter what's on the lips; it only matters what's in the heart. Only GOD knows the heart, but the Bible says that by their actions you will know them. Don't let them dis-empower you, ever.) But our fight isn't with them. And their circumstances don't concern us. Why? Because we don't have a fight. And we don't react to circumstances. We're yielded to the GOD who never changes. We worship the GOD who fights our battles *with* us and *for* us.

GOD is our Bodyguard. He is our Shield. He is our Iron Curtain of protection. He absorbs every hurtful word, every painful punch, and every deadly agenda. He absorbs it all! All the ill will that people hurl at us can't penetrate the protective wall GOD has built around our souls. He absorbs everything before it ever gets through, so that we can rest in Him.

No one can hurt you spiritually, intellectually, or emotionally unless you allow them to. That's the only way they can get through. So don't let them, OK? Repeat after me, "I do solemnly promise to relax in GOD and to allow Him to fight my fights, to dry my tears, to calm my heart, and to vindicate me. My desires are yielded to His will. And I worship Him with my life."

Thank you.

Now, go enjoy your day and walk in the confident awareness that not only is GOD on your side, but He is in fact *beside* you (and within and around you too).

Handle With Care

Sometimes you want to give people what they've got coming to them, don't you? That said, I thought I should temper my earlier comments with this advice I found in Proverbs before going to bed the other night:

"He who corrects a scoffer gets shame for himself,
    And he who rebukes a wicked man only harms himself.

Do not correct a scoffer, lest he hate you;
Rebuke a wise man, and he will love you.
Give instruction to a wise man, and he will be still wiser;
Teach a just man, and he will increase in learning" (Proverbs 9:7–9,
	NKJV).

You should figure out what this advice means to you. I hesitate to tell you what it means to me, because I don't want to stunt or influence the process of your self-discovery. Regarding the types of people I mentioned earlier who abuse us spiritually, mentally, and emotionally, we need to politely stand our ground in ways that advance GOD's purpose, and that represent Him well. We shouldn't allow people to use us as a doormat, but neither should we pick fights with them.

I think Proverbs 9 is saying that there's a kind of person who is so "dead" spiritually, so unplugged from GOD's presence, that confronting their particular areas of spiritual error would be a waste of time (because they just don't get it), and because it would only inflame them in some way and magnify their destructive intentions toward you.

Like I said, I don't want to influence you before you've had some time to think this through for yourself. Do you have some problem people in your life? Then seek GOD's counsel. After spending time in prayer and meditation, you'll know how to best handle the situation. But go to Him first, or you risk making matters worse for yourself.

Encounter the Word

Read Romans 12, and then give special attention and meditation to the following passage:

"Therefore, I urge you, brothers, in view of God's mercy, to offer your bodies as living sacrifices, holy and pleasing to God—this is your spiritual act of worship. Do not conform any longer to the pattern of this world, but be transformed by the renewing of your mind. Then you will be able to test and approve what God's will is—his good, pleasing and perfect will" (Romans 12:1, 2 NIV).

Encounter

+ Where in your life have you encountered the abusive treatment of others? What has been your typical reaction to those circumstances?

+ What discussions have you had with GOD about this treatment? How have your conversations with GOD been similar or different from Psalm 69?

+ How do you offer yourself as a "living sacrifice" to GOD and yet not allow yourself to be a doormat?

2.95 You Might Not Like This

(Lynell LaMountain)

Do you believe every person has redeemable qualities?

Some people say that even if a person is 87 percent "bad," twisted, or nutty, he or she will have at least one good quality or trait.

I'm not sure I buy into this because of people like Hitler, you know.

But here's what I can say for a fact—and this applies to the Hitlers in our world too: every person on earth is a teacher, whether they want to be or not.

Lately we've been talking about difficult people. One of the most constructive things you can do for yourself when confronted with a difficult person—with someone who abuses you emotionally, mentally, or spiritually—is to take a step back. Remove yourself from the emotion of the situation. You can do this because Psalm 46:10 says, "Relax and know that I am GOD" (paraphrase).

Once you've used GOD's power to detach emotionally, you'll have the ability to analyze the person. Why should you do this? Because there's a lesson to be learned that will strengthen or improve your life or that will decrease your pain or increase your happiness. That's what's in it for you if you do this.

Everyone you meet is a walking textbook of how to do and not to do things. Everyone. Even Hitler was. So, as you deal with the people who are driving you crazy and making life miserable for you, salvage the situation by using it as an opportunity to receive wisdom, knowledge, and understanding—especially in the area of how *not* to live, believe, behave, or treat people.

GOD's Opinion of You

We live in a world that devalues, belittles, and demeans people.

Yes, there's the occasional hero who rushes into a burning building to save someone. There are moments when people risk their lives to save strangers. But, generally, the world is indifferent about you. It doesn't love or hate you. It just doesn't care.

In my spiritual private time this morning, I came across a verse from Psalm 71 (this psalm is a picture of what the perfect earthly king would look like, but it also foretells the perfect kingly reign of the Messiah—Jesus Christ):

> For he [GOD] will deliver the needy who cry out,
>> the afflicted who have no one to help.
> He will take pity on the weak and the needy
>> and save the needy from death.
> He will rescue them from oppression and violence,
>> for precious is their blood in his sight (Psalm 72:12–14, NIV).

It's very, very important for you to get your sense of value from the right place—GOD has determined your true value. Whether or not you believe it is up to you. You are the rich child of a loving heavenly Father. You are a child of fortune, grace, and power. *You* are precious to GOD. His approval is the only approval you'll ever need. His acceptance is the only acceptance you'll ever need. His love satisfies the longings of your heart, and it makes you strong in happiness, peace, and hope.

Encounter the Word

Read Matthew 5 and then give special attention and meditation to the following passage:

This is what the LORD says:
> "The people who survive the sword
will find favor in the desert;
I will come to give rest to Israel."
The LORD appeared to us in the past, saying:
> "I have loved you with an everlasting love;
I have drawn you with loving-kindness.
I will build you up again

and you will be rebuilt, O Virgin Israel.
Again you will take up your tambourines
and go out to dance with the joyful" (Jeremiah 31:2–4, NIV).

Encounter

+ When you endure difficult circumstances, especially when it involves difficult people, where do you draw your strength from?
+ What lessons can be learned from Jesus, both in His life example and His teachings?
+ Where do you draw your hope from? How would you generate joy in the midst of life's challenges?
+ What have your most difficult relationships taught you? What has GOD offered to you in those life lessons?

My Experience

_____

_____

_____

_____

_____

_____

_____

_____

_____

_____

_____

_____

_____

_____

_____

3.0 GOSPEL

3.1 Be Agents of Present Gospel

It is our desire to experience the power of GOD's everlasting gospel. We're learning, again or for the first time, the good news that kingdom living begins now. Today is one more day in eternity, and I live in that new reality.

3.2 Resolute

(Shayna Bailey)

"I don't think that GOD can forgive me."[1]

Sessa's friend, Sienna, was sitting at our dining-room table. Rows of perfectly cut sugar cookies were aligned on the dark cherry-wood finish in front of her. Looking up from delicately applying brightly colored frosting, she continued.

"I'm having an affair with a married man."

Sienna didn't know that Sessa had already told me about Jason. She was tired and exasperated with Sienna and the sexual addiction she claimed was driving her behavior. When Sienna would call to complain about her own marriage being in shambles, Sessa would listen. Then she would come into my room to vent her frustration. I had been hearing a running update on Jason for weeks already.

"Sienna, GOD can forgive anything," I confidently informed her. "We all make mistakes."

---

1. Original date of entry was January 1, 2007.

"Yeah, right," Sienna responded. She looked very pointedly at me before continuing. "What about you?" she asked. "What have you done wrong?"

I had just finished talking to my friend, Manuel, about a spiritual hurdle he was facing. Earlier, we were eating dinner when Sessa and Sienna had walked into the apartment, and afterwards, while I mixed and formed Christmas cookies in the kitchen, Manuel had hovered close by, talking. Sessa and Sienna could hear our conversation, and I surmised that it was what sparked the current question about forgiveness.

"Tell me something that you've done that you knew was wrong," Sienna pressed.

Sessa was looking up at me from the dining-room table. She raised her eyebrows in encouragement.

"Well," I started. "Remember how I told you that some things happened with David that shouldn't have?"

Sienna's eyes widened.

"I was living with David for two months."

I was already looking away, and I wanted to stop talking. Such a revelation may not have seemed especially provocative in light of Sienna's current situation, but my heart was beating furiously, and I was sweating.

"I don't believe in premarital sex, Sienna. I try to hold myself to a different standard. But last year when the house I was living in flooded, I made a decision that I knew was wrong. I could have moved into my pastor's house, I could have moved in with a friend, and I even could have moved home to Florida. But I didn't. I moved in with David because I wanted to."

Sienna was still looking up at me, awaiting the sinful revelation.

"We never actually had intercourse, but . . . "

"Don't let her pressure you into telling more than you want to!" Sessa interrupted defensively.

"Things went further than they should have."

I knew I was incapable of advising Sienna on something as serious as a sexual addiction. So I continued with the most honest answer I could give. "GOD not only forgives us, but He blesses us when we remove the known sin from our lives."

I didn't want to sound too preachy or judgmental, so I shared what had been very real struggles for me. It was hard to move out. I almost went broke paying the rent on my two-bedroom apartment before Sessa moved in. David was frustrated when he couldn't understand why I would choose to scrape by on my own, when he was offering me residence in his spacious three-bedroom house for free. But GOD did forgive me. He also blessed me. First, I had to take myself out of the situation though.

Within a few months of moving out of David's house, my promotion at work took off. Then I found a roommate to split the bills with. I applied for a per diem hospital job that I really wanted and got it. My relationship with my mother improved markedly (probably because I was no longer lying about my living situation), and so did my other interpersonal relationships. Most important, though, the struggles that David and I had been having subsided. He understood my convictions once I was brave enough to demonstrate what they were. Eventually, the pressure for a physical relationship started decreasing too. I even heard David correct a friend once after he had a made a raucous joke about our relationship. "It's not like that, man. She's a virgin." He sounded proud, and I was surprised that he hadn't glossed over the comment or let it slide without correction.

I did make mistakes, and there are a lot of things that could use improvement in my life. I need to be a better friend. I need to be less selfish. I need to talk about things that I'm ashamed of if they will encourage someone else.

More than anything, though, I just need to be more faithful. I always whine, cry, and despair when GOD is leading me in a direction I don't want to go in. I can never see the end when I'm at the beginning, and I chronically fear the worst. So, of everything I could offer God, my resolution is wrapped up in the desire to believe more deeply, more simply, and with more conviction. Everything else will come with it.

Encounter the Word

"Who is a God like you, who pardons sin and forgives the transgression of the remnant of his inheritance? You do not stay angry forever but delight to show mercy. You will again have compassion on us; you will tread our sins underfoot and hurl all our iniquities into the depths of the sea" (Micah 7:18, 19, NIV).

Encounter

* What is preventing you from living freely in GOD's grace? What sins continue to bind you?
* Where do you believe GOD cannot go? What is beyond GOD's ability to forgive?
* What are you unable to forgive yourself for? How might you follow GOD's example of forgiveness?
* Whom do you need to authentically ask for forgiveness? Might you need to ask yourself for forgiveness? Elaborate on why.
* What step will you take today, with GOD, to begin living more faithfully?

3.3 Signed, Sealed, and Delivered

(Denise Badger)

I have a particular affinity for seals, and it started young. Growing up in Montana, you don't find much to do once you finish plowing the fields, so you put food in cans, which is called canning (actually, you use mason jars, and cans aren't involved at all—go figure).

At age five, I learned that in canning, if you failed to seal the jar lid on tight, things went very badly. Come winter, the bacteria that snuck in under the lid and had a party with the peaches during the months they were sitting on a shelf nets you rotten, disgusting, unidentifiable contents that you wouldn't offer to your worst enemy. But, if you did it right, the way canning is supposed to happen— sterilized jar, filled to the top, and with the lid sealed tightly so no air gets through—then you were guaranteed to eat like a king in the winter. And that guarantee was definitely worth the wait.

Fast-forward to fifth grade, and meet my best friend, Marce. We were kindred spirits. Deeply devoted as only ten-year-olds can be, we decided to forever seal our friendship with a solemn oath. We packed a picnic, found a park with a stream, stood teetering on two rocks in the middle of the water, clasped hands, and repeated words of undying love, sealing our friendship forever. It was a guaranteed, sure thing. Eighteen years and memories later, I stood in her wedding and felt the deep satisfaction of a true and lasting friendship.

And then there was the time when a seal saved my life. In 1998 . . . a sailing trip to the Bahamas . . . rough waters, a weak swimmer with a healthy dose of "But I can do this!" One-hundred-fifty yards from the boat and my asthma kicks in. Frozen airways, one scream for help, and then I see my husband, just like the hero in the movies, dive off the boat and swim to save me. His arms circled about me, sealing me to him as he dragged me back to safety. His arms kept me to him, kept me afloat, and kept me alive.

But, by far, the best seal of all is found in Ephesians 1:13, 14. It says that GOD, the Holy Spirit, is our Seal, guaranteeing our salvation! Just like the canning seal, the Holy Spirit keeps us from eating the rotten stuff sin offers. Like the seal of friendship, the Holy Spirit keeps us connected to GOD, deepening our friendship through time and experiences together. And like the seal of life-saving arms, the Holy Spirit puts His arms around us and takes us to safety through trials of life over and over again, ultimately setting our feet on heavenly ground, safe for eternity.

Can the seal be broken? Yeah, it can. But Hebrews 13:5 says it will never be GOD who breaks away. When we accept and choose Him as our personal Savior and Friend for life, that's exactly what we get . . . for life, for eternity. It's sealed! It's guaranteed!

Encounter the Word

Read Ephesians 1, and then give special attention and meditation to the following passage:

"And you also were included in Christ when you heard the word of truth, the gospel of your salvation. Having believed, you were marked in him with a seal, the promised Holy Spirit, who is a deposit guaranteeing our inheritance until the redemption of those who are God's possession—to the praise of his glory" (Ephesians 1:13, 14, NIV).

Encounter

- Have you said Yes to GOD, to His seal in your life, guaranteeing your eternity with Him? If yes, thank Him right now for such an incredible promise and guarantee. If not, what are you waiting for?
- Seal Assessment: Is there any rotten stuff in your life that you need the

Holy Spirit to get rid of? How's the strength of your friendship with GOD—any area need to be tightened up? Where in your life do you need to scream, "Help!" to GOD and let Him get you through? His arms are ready to keep holding tight and get you through, if you let Him . . . it's a sealed promise!

3.4 Gone in Twenty Minutes

(Sam McKee)

With all the bright sunshine and blue skies, the day just seemed too perfect and picturesque to include any real danger. The strong wind was churning up white-capped waves to match the billowy clouds racing by above Lake Michigan. My dad's Siberian huskies were gracefully sprinting along the shoreline, chasing Frisbees and dodging the waves. It was the end of the last of my youthful summers.

Graduation behind me and a youth pastor job in Colorado before me, I was enjoying a carefree day at the beach with my dad and three friends. What a stark contrast to the last half of that afternoon. I never felt more hopeless or close to death in my whole life.

The wind was gusting, and the waves were curling over as I'd never seen before. Sometimes the Great Lakes[2] can muster up swells of five to eight feet, drawing surfers even from Chicago. On occasion, rip currents can violently pull novices out into deep water. The cold water can sap a swimmer's strength, and the waves can pound them right into the sea walls or the rocky shoreline.

After running the dogs on the beach, we headed toward the lighthouse. On each side of the cement pier was a ten-foot drop-off with a metal sea wall. As we walked along, we saw some teenagers bouncing up and down on the incredible surf. The three- to four-foot waves were crashing into the sea wall and surging together like a huge wave pool at an amusement park. It looked like so much fun that I wanted to jump in with them. One of the teenagers, a heavy-set guy, waved at us.

After taking pictures at the lighthouse, we started walking back. While we

---

2. A group of five large lakes in North America on and near the Canada-United States border.

were still on the part of the pier above very deep water, I started hearing a faint call: "Help . . . help." I looked over the edge of the sea wall and saw the heavy-set teenager being tossed around by the surging waters. So I kicked off my sandals and jumped in.

The rip current had pulled him out about 150 yards from shore, and the chilly waters were sapping his strength. As I came up to the surface, I found the 225-pound teenager. By this time, he was very lethargic and short of breath. I went under and tried pushing him up so he could get some more air, but only the top of his head came out of the water. The water was deep, and the waves were pouring over us. Every time I pushed him up, he didn't go up enough to get a full breath. At the same time, he was going into shock and trying to grab hold of my arms. I was being pulled down by him and not getting much air myself. He was so lethargic that he could barely tread water.

I looked up at the huge, dark sea wall ten feet above us and couldn't see a ladder in either direction. The waves were surging, and they seemed ready at any moment to lift us up in their palms and pound us into the mossy metal wall.

My greatest fears were before me. I couldn't shake the thought that I, and also this kid, might not make it out of the water alive.

We'll leave that story hanging in midair for a few moments, while you ponder the question: What if your life was gone in twenty minutes?

Have You Been There?

Have you ever had a scare like I did? A brush with death? A test result comes back with a question mark; a lab reading throws a red flag; a tumor strikes a chord of terror; a truck blows a red light; the earth quakes, the lightning strikes, your heart skips a beat, and your mortality is suddenly before you as never before.

In one Gallup poll, the top two fears of Americans were (1) public speaking and (2) death.[3] It's worth noting that those two fears are the main ways that the Christian church grew so rapidly in the beginning. It was through the preaching of the apostles and the blood of the martyrs. Tertullian wrote that the blood of the martyrs was the "seed of the Church." One Christian would bravely die in the

---

3. Seinfeld joked that at any given funeral, people would rather be in the casket than giving the eulogy.

Colosseum, and three or four converts would pop up in their place, amazed at a faith that could stare death in the face—and smile.

GOD wants us to face death squarely and early, so we can live wisely. The Bible says our life is a mist. "You do not know what your life will be like tomorrow. You are just a vapor that appears for a little while and then vanishes away" (James 4:14, NASB).

It is here today and gone tomorrow. It is here now and gone in a moment.

Almost every minute, someone in the United States will die from a coronary event.[4] And two people around the world will die every minute in a car accident.[5] That's 3,287 deaths per day, 1.2 million per year.

What if you were gone in twenty minutes? What if you didn't have time to do anything else, not even make another call? What would be your top three regrets? What loose ends would you leave untied? When you answer those questions, you'll probably find the priorities that have slipped into lower places.

Imagining the End

Although it seems morbid, David said it's a wonderful blessing to look at the brevity of life. In Psalm 90 he wrote, "Teach us to number our days aright, that we may gain a heart of wisdom" (verse 12, NIV). Or as Max Lucado renders it: "Teach us how short our lives really are, so that we may be wise." The breath you have is precious, but it is passing. Our time on earth is always ticking away, always becoming shorter.

For one week a while back, I'd say every morning out loud, "This may be my last day." I did this every morning for a week and almost drove my wife nuts. But I had a great week. The trivial things that normally angered me or made me critical were nothing. After all, this was my last day on earth, so why would I want to let some lousy driver or some minor misfortune ruin it? And why would I want to be critical of my family and friends, when this was my last day to speak with them?

And as I went through a busy day of work and ministry, I noticed the typical foolish resentment and complaining was absent from my mind. This was my last

---

4. Stanford University Medical Center. December 19, 2008. http://www.stanfordhospital.com/healthLib/atoz/cardiac/stats.html.

5. World Report on Road Traffic Injury Prevention, April 7, 2004.

day to make a difference for the kingdom—why would I want to spend it licking my wounds or whining about not having quail?

There's something about death that shrinks the trivial and enlarges the important. It distills our priorities. One friend of our family found out shortly before her wedding that her husband had a terminal illness. This couple knew they only had a short time together, so they cut out all those foolish toothpaste and toilet-paper arguments that we typical newlyweds, and even oldie-weds, wallow in. They knew their time was short, so they seized every moment and filled it to the brim with love. Their five years together were filled with the equivalent of fifty years of memories and romance.

Jesus was like that. He packed much into His brief life on earth. He seems like the type who laughed hard at people's jokes, cried at people's pain, danced at people's weddings, played hard, prayed hard, and tapped every single ounce of glory out of each day.

You can just hear someone asking Jesus, "So what did You do last week?" Jesus, being humble, says, "Oh, you know, the same old stuff." One of His disciples pipes up, "Yeah, He just walked on water, stopped a hurricane, healed a leper, had a blast at a wedding feast, hiked a mountain, preached a sermon, prayed with a soldier, went fishing, went sailing, took a long nap in the boat, and prayed at dawn and at dusk each day."

John said that if someone tried to write down all the things that Jesus did, there wouldn't be enough room in the world for all the books they'd fill.

And yet, even with that clock ticking, Jesus never seemed to be in a hurry. (A spiritual mentor told John Ortberg that his one action item for spiritual growth was to "ruthlessly eliminate hurry from your life.")[6] With Jesus' short life, His hectic schedule, the most important start-up company and the most important job in all of history, He was never too busy to pray. Maybe that's why He reached all His goals. He knew why He was here. He knew where the real power was. He knew that life was too short to waste a moment without GOD the Father.

GOD wants you to have some incredible things to talk about when your days are over, and He wants you to have no regrets.

---

6. *Leadership Magazine*, July 4, 2002.

What are the priorities you want to have at the center of your life? If you had only twenty minutes to live, how would you finish these statements?

1. I need to thank . . .

"One of them, when he saw he was healed, came back, praising God in a loud voice. He threw himself at Jesus' feet and thanked him" (Luke 17:15, 16a, NIV).

2. I need to forgive . . .

"Forgive as the Lord forgave you" (Colossians 3:13, NIV).

3. I need to make peace with . . .

"Do not let the sun set on your anger" (Ephesians 4:26, NASB).

4. I need to do something nice for . . .

"Whatever you did for one of the least of these . . . you did for me" (Matthew 25:40, NIV).

5. I need to share GOD's love and my faith with . . .

"Pray that every time I open my mouth I'll be able to make Christ plain as day to them. . . . Make the most of every opportunity" (Colossians 4:4, 5, *The Message*).

How It Ended

That huge teenage guy in deep water with crashing waves all around him really needed an Olympic swimmer that day. Instead he got someone with the build of a Ping-Pong player. I felt like neither of us was going to survive.

Have you ever noticed that emergencies have a way of eliminating the fluff from your prayers? I started praying, *Jesus, Jesus, come and help us. Come, Jesus, come.* And with that, I felt a new burst of energy and strength within me. I pushed the teenager to the sea wall and hoped he could get a grip there. I hoisted him up, but his hands only slid down the slick metal. The waves were pushing us back and forth. I was hoping they wouldn't crash us into the wall. I looked up and saw my friend on top of the sea wall, and asked her where the nearest ladder was. She pointed toward the deeper water. So I yelled to the guy for him to start kicking his legs. We pushed and kicked and splashed our way against the waves until we found the ladder and made it to safety on the pier.

Although several people drown there each year, we made it out alive. When I got up on top of the walkway, he came and thanked me. He said, "You saved my life." He was looking at me like he couldn't believe I had helped him. With my eyes bloodshot from the stress, I said something like, "Hey, man, that wasn't about me. Look at my biceps. You could floss your teeth with these puppies. Jesus cares about you, and He wanted you to live, so He saved us."

A few minutes later, he chased after me and said, "Hey, what church do you go to?"

I was happy to tell him. And a couple weeks later, when I preached my last sermon in Illinois, he was there, receiving his invitation to a life that never ends.

This teenager and I survived a brush with death, just as you have survived these twenty minutes. Whether you're gone in twenty minutes, or gone in twenty years, the question for all of us is: "What will we do with the time we have left?" You never know when it will end.[7]

Encounter the Word

After reading John 10:1–18, give special attention and meditation to the following passages:

"Since the children have flesh and blood, he too shared in their humanity so that by his death he might destroy him who holds the power of death—that is, the devil—and free those who all their lives were held in slavery by their fear of death" (Hebrews 2:14, 15, NIV).

"The thief comes only to steal and kill and destroy; I have come that they may have life, and have it to the full" (John 10:10, NIV).

Encounter

+ If today was your last day, what would you celebrate? How would it be different?
+ Whom do you need to thank? To forgive? To make peace with?
+ Who can you do something nice for? Whom do you need to share your faith with?
+ How might you "seize the day" today?

---

7. This entry originally appeared in *Adventist Review*, November 9, 2006, 24–26. Reprinted with permission.

3.5 The Reach of Grace

(Lynell LaMountain)

Have you ever profoundly regretted anything you've done? Something so awful that it affected you deeply? We've all done things we regret, and sometimes we've done them so often, we wonder if we're beyond the reach of grace.

We live with waves of guilt . . .

Moments of shame . . .

Crushing self-condemnation . . .

Asking ourselves, "Why, why, why?"

"If only I had done that differently . . . if only I had not gone there . . . if only I had said that instead . . ."

Many people live with secret burdens of things done or left undone, of things said or left unsaid. They would pay any price for a time machine to make it right.

But they can't.

And so they live with a wound in their soul that's raw, tender, and cold—a reminder of their deepest failure(s).

I was reading about King David's battle with this in Psalm 51. In case you don't know, David had an adulterous affair with a woman named Bathsheba. She got pregnant.

David had her husband, a soldier, brought back from the front lines to be with Bathsheba, so that people would naturally assume the child was conceived by him. But, Bathsheba's husband wouldn't go home. His country was at war, and he believed his place was beside his king, whom he had sworn to protect. So he stayed in the royal court.

David returned him to the front lines and instructed the general to deploy him in the battle where death was certain. David murdered Bathsheba's husband, then took her to be his wife in order to cover up their adulterous affair and pregnancy.

As time wore on, David wore down. Crushed by guilt, shame, and regret, his sins were grinding his bones into a bitter powder. But as hopeless as he felt, grace reached for him (you can read about in Psalm 51).

If grace can reach an adulterer and murderer like David, then it can reach someone like you with a past like yours. No matter what you've done or how you've lived, grace is reaching for you.

How do I know?

Because you're reading this right now. (You didn't think you were reading this by accident, did you?) Grace blots out your mistakes, washes away your regret, and removes any life-lessening or life-depleting thoughts and beliefs from your life. Grace picks up the broken pieces of your life and puts them back together, and in putting them back together, it makes you one with GOD again.

Despite what David had done, GOD considered him His friend. And, through it all, GOD never loved David any less. Same holds true for you.

Encounter the Word

After reading all of chapter 2 in Ephesians, give special attention and meditation to the following passages:

"This righteousness from God comes through faith in Jesus Christ to all who believe. There is no difference, for all have sinned and fall short of the glory of God, and are justified freely by his grace through the redemption that came by Christ Jesus" (Romans 3:22–24, NIV).

"In order that in the coming ages he might show the incomparable riches of his grace, expressed in his kindness to us in Christ Jesus. For it is by grace you have been saved, through faith—and this not from yourselves, it is the gift of GOD—not by works, so that no one can boast" (Ephesians 2:7–9, NIV).

Encounter

+ Where in your life do you desire GOD's grace to be applied?
+ How fond do you imagine GOD is of you? What do you believe can diminish His fondness?
+ What do you sense GOD doing to reach out to you?

3.55 Oneness

(Lynell LaMountain)

Oneness with GOD. What does that mean to you?

For someone who believes GOD is demanding and hard to please, oneness with Him might mean a life of misery.

For someone who believes GOD is on his or her side, that He wants him or her to be free, full of life, and overflowing with joy, oneness with Him would be a state of sublime spiritual bliss, right?

King David believed the latter.

In Psalm 51, he asked for three things that made Him one with GOD and that we can ask for today:

1. "Create in me a pure heart" (Verse 10, NIV).

Remember, out of David's heart came an adulterous affair with Bathsheba and premeditated murder. He was truly remorseful and desired change. This required a new heart.

Change, no matter what it is, begins on the inside.

2. "Renew a steadfast spirit within me" (Verse 10, NIV).

Not only did David want a new heart, he wanted to stay the course. Because even though GOD gave him a new heart, GOD didn't remove his free will.

3. "Restore to me the joy of your salvation" (Verse 12, NIV).

David wanted to experience spiritual intimacy with GOD again. Because of his affair with Bathsheba, and murderous scheme, he had lost intimacy with GOD. And he wanted it back. The only way he could get it back was by GOD's transforming grace, which was something David wanted to experience more than his next breath. From what David wrote in Psalm 51, we learn that oneness with GOD results from:

1. a new heart (which GOD gives);
2. a steadfast spirit (which GOD gives);
3. and joy (which GOD gives).

GOD is reaching for us. We're not beyond the reach of grace.

If GOD was interested in judging and condemning us, He could've stayed where He was, leaving us to our secret moments of misery.

GOD, your heavenly Father, wants to be one with you.

Why?

Because He likes you.

And because He wants to empower you to be free and happy, and transform you into the beautiful person you're destined to become in Him.

Encounter the Word

"I will give you a new heart and put a new spirit in you; I will remove from you your heart of stone and give you a heart of flesh. And I will put my Spirit in you and move you to follow my decrees and be careful to keep my laws" (Ezekiel 36:26, 27, NIV).

Encounter

+ When it comes to GOD, what is your heart's desire?
+ What changes are happening for you internally to foster a closer relationship with GOD?
+ How is GOD transforming your heart from stone to flesh? In other words, how is He making you more vulnerable to His love?

3.6 Yuck

(Lynell LaMountain)

Forgiveness. Yuck.

I know it's difficult to forgive someone—boy, do I ever know—especially when you feel that you have a justifiable cause to hold a grudge, and, in your mind, you've been hanging them in effigy.

But . . .

Bitterness. Grudges. Resentment. These emotions strain our joy and fracture our happiness. I read something today that prompted this entry:

"Resentment is like drinking poison and expecting the other person to die."

For your own good, don't drink the poisonous water of resentment. Ephesians 4:31, 32 says, "Make a clean break with all cutting, backbiting, profane talk. Be gentle with one another, sensitive. Forgive one another as quickly and thoroughly as God in Christ forgave you" (*The Message*).

Why I should I forgive?

1. Because I'll be happier.
2. Because I'll be more successful.
3. Because I've been forgiven.
4. Because grudges will destroy me eventually.

If you can't find it within yourself to forgive someone, then maybe praying this prayer will help: "Jesus within me forgives _____ (person's name) for _____ (what he or she did)." Praying this prayer has helped me overcome certain joy-depleting situations and toxic relationships.

If you're bold and are willing to try something even more daring, you might pray this prayer (when you're ready): "Jesus within me blesses _____ (person's name) with joy and prosperity."

Why pray a prayer like this for a person you don't feel deserves it? Because our thoughts and words have demonstrable power—they manifest things. They get results! With our words we either bless or curse. And the Bible teaches that if we bless, our lives will become blessed, but if we curse, our lives will become cursed.

It goes back to that old adage, "You reap what you sow."

Today, one of the greatest gifts you can give is the gift of forgiveness. You don't even have to tell the person that you forgave them. Just pray the prayers I gave you for a few days, weeks, and months and see what happens.

Maybe the person you need to forgive most is yourself. And that's a great place to start. Need some help? Then this promise is for you: "On the other hand, if we admit our sins—make a clean break of them—he won't let us down; he'll be true to himself. He'll forgive our sins and purge us of all wrongdoing" (1 John 1:9, *The Message*).

Encounter the Word

Read Luke 6:27–49, and then give special attention and meditation to the following passage:

"But love your enemies, do good to them, and lend to them without expecting to get anything back. Then your reward will be great, and you will be sons of the Most High, because he is kind to the ungrateful and wicked. Be merciful, just as your Father is merciful" (Luke 6:35, 36, NIV).

Encounter

+ What is "poisoning" your life right now? How is resentment or bitterness sapping away your joy?
+ Who is eligible for your forgiveness prayer? What is preventing you from praying the prayer for them right now?

◆ How good is GOD's forgiveness? What might life be like, poison-free?

3.7 Porn for Bibles

(Lynell LaMountain)

How people respond to finding valuable things always interests me, because their response is a profound insight into the human condition, especially theirs.

A Los Angeles cab driver, Haider Sediqi, found $350,000 in diamonds that had been left in the backseat of his cab by a New York jeweler, who subsequently rewarded him with $10,000, a diamond bracelet, and a Thank-you note—which, according to Sediqi, meant just as much to him as the reward (and, for some reason, I believe him). Apparently, the jeweler told him in the Thank-you note that this act of honesty and integrity had changed his life.

Eric Austin left the diamonds in the cab when he got out at the Los Angeles airport. Sediqi tracked him down through a cell phone bill that he found in the bag of diamonds.

Although Austin had promised the cab driver a reward, Sediqi didn't give it much thought until it actually arrived. What did he do with it?

He gave the bracelet to his wife, Nasima, and said that he would use the money to pay for his children's schooling.[8]

To me, the Bible is my "bag" of diamonds—and although I've studied it all my life and have a BA in religion and a master of divinity degree, in some ways, I feel like it's been only recently that I'm understanding its beautiful, life-enriching truths. Proverbs 16:16 says, "How much better to get wisdom than gold, to choose understanding rather than silver!" (NIV). The Bible contains the empowering principles of life, joy, purpose, and love. Within its pages is the formula for living and being happy.

When my plane was flying through the storm clouds and landing in Jacksonville the other night, there came a point when the fog lifted and I could see where we were going. That's how truth works. And that's been my experience with the Bible. I wouldn't trade it for all the diamonds in the world.

Now, imagine my surprise when I read an article[9] that my friend e-mailed me.

---

8. Adapted from a story in *USA Today*, December 1, 2005.

9. http://www.msnbc.msn.com/id/10349028.

Ready for the headline? "Trading Bibles for Porn in San Antonio."

Apparently, a collegiate atheist group is trading Bibles for porn. It claims that the Bible is being misused.

We all know that the Bible has been misused, abused, and misinterpreted through the years. It's unfortunate. But then the writer of the article said something that gave me an interesting insight into the human condition, especially his: he said that the Bible contradicts itself on every page.

And I wondered, *How would he even know?* Because that statement proves that he's never even cracked the cover. If anything is filled with contradiction, it's his heart, because we are what we cherish most, and what we believe.

And then I remembered something Jesus said in Matthew 7:6: "Do not give what is holy to the dogs; nor cast your pearls before swine, lest they trample them under their feet, and turn and tear you in pieces" (NIV).

Albert Einstein said this: "Not everything that can be counted counts, and not everything that counts can be counted."

Not everything is as it seems. And life is too important to be written off with such casual disregard. Many things are being said and taught about the Bible today. I don't know what your beliefs are, and I don't want to preach to you. But if there was ever a time to know what you personally believe and why you believe it, it's now. And I would like to suggest for your consideration that the Bible will take you places your heart has always dreamed of . . . all you have to do is believe.

Encounter the Word

After reading chapter 119 of Psalms, give special attention and meditation to the following passage:

"How can a young person live a clean life? By carefully reading the map of your Word. I'm single-minded in pursuit of you; don't let me miss the road signs you've posted. I've banked your promises in the vault of my heart so I won't sin myself bankrupt" (Psalm 119: 9–11, *The Message*).

Encounter

+ What guides your life? How do you come to decisions regarding behavior, relationships, and goals?
+ What role would you like for GOD's Word to play in your life decisions?

+ What other guidebooks for life have you considered? Elaborate on your experience(s).

3.75 John 3:17

(Lynell LaMountain)

I think that a lot of Christians give Jesus and GOD a bad rap. Especially GOD. I know this doesn't apply to you, but many Christians in the past have described GOD as angry—angry at us and with us—and that Christ died to make GOD's anger go away.

Not true!

Christ didn't have to appease GOD by dying because:

1. GOD didn't need appeasing, and,
2. His death wasn't about appeasing.

Here's the deal: sin doesn't equal bad things/immorality. Sin = death. There's one Source of life in the universe, and that's GOD. Apart from this Source, there's only death. Severed from this Source, we die.

Here's what Jesus did on the cross: He allowed the inevitable conclusion of our choice to be fully manifested in His life—which meant death for Him, just as it would've meant for us.

It wasn't that He died for the bad things that we do in order to appease an angry, vengeful GOD. Absolutely not. He switched places with me and allowed the consequences of my choice to do to His life what it would've done to my life. As a member of the human family (thanks to Adam and Eve), by default (I know it doesn't sound fair) I was born separated—out of fellowship with GOD.

On the cross, Jesus took upon Himself my separation and gave me His fellowship—His oneness with GOD—grafting me back into GOD's family. On the cross, Jesus *became* my separation from GOD, which resulted in His death because separation from Life equals death.

That's how I understand it, and that's my imperfect explanation.

"For God did not send His Son into the world to condemn the world, but that the world through Him might be saved" (John 3:17, NIV).

We have a loving heavenly Father who cares for us in every way and who can't wait to reunite His family—us—where we'll enjoy one another forever in His gracious presence.

Encounter the Word

"Surely he took up our infirmities and carried our sorrows, yet we considered him stricken by God, smitten by him, and afflicted. But he was pierced for our transgressions, he was crushed for our iniquities; the punishment that brought us peace was upon him, and by his wounds we are healed. We all, like sheep, have gone astray, each of us has turned to his own way; and the LORD has laid on him the iniquity of us all" (Isaiah 53:4–6, NIV).

Encounter

- ✦ What is your perception of GOD? How does Jesus fit into the mix between you and GOD?
- ✦ If you accept Jesus' offer and are reconnected to GOD and life through Him, what does that mean for you today?
- ✦ What can you do to change the "rap" that is being given to GOD and to Jesus?

3.8 Committed

(Shayna Bailey)

I thought I'd start today's blog with a little blatant self-revelation.[10] You should know that I have commitment issues. Not the kind that you think, though.

I have commitment issues with GOD.

Don't get me wrong. I like the concept of unconditional love. Realistically, though, love always comes with conditions—at least in my world. I know that my parents and family love me, but I also know which life choices displease them, so I avoid those. I also know that in my dating relationships, there will be conditions placed upon me. After all, I definitely place them on my significant others.

So how does this relate to GOD?

---

10. This entry was blogged September 12, 2005.

Well, imperfect, conditional love has trained me to expect rejection when I fall short. Since I am sinful, though, I *always* fall short in my relationship with GOD. When I do, I expect judgment and wrath. I fear ensuing punishment. I start to doubt that GOD still intends to bless me in my weakness. *GOD's unconditional love is just too good to be true.*

My weak and tired response is what it always is when I feel rejection coming: I pull away first. Rather than wait for the hellfire and damnation, I get out of the way and hide. I wrap myself up in my shame and convince myself that GOD is as disappointed in me as I am in myself.

Unfortunately, distancing myself from GOD seals off the blessings that He has in store for me. I miss the lessons intended to teach me, and I waste time trying to figure out how to restore my relationship after I finally realize the sky isn't going to fall.

My commitment issues with GOD are *completely* self-defeating.

Psalms 103:8 reminds us that GOD is "compassionate and gracious," "slow to anger," and "abounding in love" (NIV). *Um . . . where's the judgment and wrath part again?* We are told that He doesn't punish us as we sometimes deserve (see verse 10). Rather, we're assured that He has compassion on us and "remembers that we are [only] dust" (verse 14).

Romans 8:38 says, "Neither death nor life, neither angels nor demons, neither the present nor the future, nor any powers, neither height nor depth, nor anything else in all creation, will be able to separate us from the love of GOD that is in Christ Jesus our Lord" (NIV). It gives me comfort to know that even when I get scared, pull away, or just feel distant and unworthy, GOD's still committed to me. Nothing can separate me from His love even when I deserve to be rejected.

Have you had commitment issues lately?

Encounter the Word

"He does not treat us as our sins deserve or repay us according to our iniquities. For as high as the heavens are above the earth, so great is his love for those who fear him; as far as the east is from the west, so far has he removed our transgressions from us. As a father has compassion on his children, so the Lord has compassion on those who fear him; for he knows how we are formed, he remembers that we are dust" (Psalm 103:10–14, NIV).

Encounter

+ What are the pros and cons of commitment? How does this apply to relationships? To GOD?
+ Where in your life do you depend on commitment? What would commitment to GOD mean to you?
+ How do you perceive GOD's level of commitment to you? Have you talked with GOD about this?

3.9 You Rule

(Lynell LaMountain)

I have some very important advice for you today, and here it is:

Never invalidate yourself. Never! Got it? Good.

In GOD's eyes, you are worthy, deserving, and valuable. You mean something to Him. He treasures you. He created you, redeemed you, restored you, and secured you for eternity.

There are many people in this world today, including family members, colleagues, friends, and "religious" people, who say and do things to invalidate you. After a while, for whatever reasons, we believe them. Since we don't measure up to their standards—whether those standards are educational, social, financial, or religious—we invalidate ourselves by thinking *and* believing we're not worthy, or deserving, or important.

In the words of that great theologian, Scrooge, "Bah, humbug!"

You are *not* a worm. You are *not* an insignificant piece of dust. You are *not* a worthless piece of junk that's been forgotten inside a dusty box in the cosmos' cobwebby attic.

Absolutely *not*!

What are you? This: "When I consider your [GOD's] heavens, the work of your fingers, the moon and the stars, which you have set in place, what is man that you are mindful of him, the son of man that you care for him? You made him a little lower than the heavenly beings and crowned him with glory and honor. You made him ruler over the works of your hands; you put everything under his feet" (Psalm 8:3–6, NIV).

What are you? A coruler with GOD.

Invalidating yourself is a sin, because, in doing so, you're blaspheming the handiwork of GOD. So don't do it, OK? Repeat after me: "I am the rich child of a loving heavenly Father who delights in me."

Coruler?

A coruler with GOD? How does that work? There are many ways. But here's one: find a promise in the Bible that relates to your situation and desire and then *claim* it as a *present* reality and not as a *future* wish (this concept is modeled in Psalm 31).

David claimed and affirmed GOD's promise for deliverance and vindication as a present reality. He claimed protection and safety in GOD now, as if it had already happened. GOD's promises aren't for some future world; they are for your world now.

In being a coruler with GOD, however, you are professing and confessing that you and GOD are like-minded—that you are one with Him. He has first place in your life. And you consider Him to be your GOD of truth. In Him, you place implicit trust. It's a relationship of absolute surrender and reliance.

David says in Psalm 31:5, "Into your hands I commit my spirit; redeem me, O Lord, the God of truth" (NIV). There's a depth to this commitment that we often overlook, because David isn't saying, "GOD, keep me from dying." He's saying, "Father GOD, even if I die, I commit my spirit into Your hands, that even in dying, I won't stay dead, for I am imperishable in your resurrecting, life-giving power."

What's David really saying? This: although he is a coruler with GOD and has dominion, and claims GOD's promises as a present reality, he commits his will to GOD and even to the extent of things not working out as he desires, believing they work out as they should. Knowing this, he lives in triumphant expectation and expresses grateful praise to GOD, His fortified castle on a tall mountain.

Claiming Promises

The power of claiming promises as a present reality, not as a future wish, is one way we corule with GOD. I'm sure you know how this works. But to ensure clarity, here's an example:

Instead of praying, "Lord, please deliver me from this situation," you would pray, "Thank You, Lord, for delivering me from this situation." In this prayer, you're affirming GOD's active presence in your life, as you actively respond to His leading.

That said, there are a number of promises that I claim daily. I'm constantly getting new ones from my studies. And one of my favorite things is sharing them with you.

"Those who know your name will trust in you, for you, O Lord, have never forsaken those who seek you" (Psalm 9:10, NIV).

"I love you Lord, O my strength. The Lord is my rock, my fortress, my deliverer; my God is my rock in whom I take refuge. He is my shield and the horn of my salvation, my stronghold. I call to the Lord, who is worthy of praise, and I am saved from my enemies" (Psalm 18:1–3, NIV).

These two promises comfort me because I'm reminded that GOD is my Source of protection, security, prosperity, and success. And that He's always there for me. I'm also reminded that the responsibility for an abundant life rests in GOD's hands, not mine.

What effect does this have on me? My peace is replenished, my strength is renewed, and my hope is established.

Practice this kind of praying and see the difference it makes in your life.

Encounter the Word

"And those he predestined, he also called; those he called, he also justified; those he justified, he also glorified. What, then, shall we say in response to this? If God is for us, who can be against us? He who did not spare his own Son, but gave him up for us all—how will he not also, along with him, graciously give us all things?" (Romans 8:30–32, NIV).

Encounter

+ What effect does ruling with GOD have on you?
+ How can you approach each day, knowing you are on GOD's side?
+ Kingdom living begins right now. How will you live this next day in eternity?

4.0 **GRACE**

4.1 *Grace*-fully Express Compassion

It is our desire to share the eternal reality of GOD's grace. We're learning to live in GOD's grace in every area of life—focusing on helping each other experience GOD's grace in all human relationships and social structures. Compassion is the ethos of Christlike community.

4.2 Crossing Jordan

(Sam Leonor)

Let's enter into Joshua 1. Did you bring your Bible? Yeah, that's what I like to hear. You can't have an encounter with GOD without having your Bible. That's the revealed Word of GOD, friend. If you didn't bring one, then fake it. Take out a hymnal, or something.

After the death of Moses, the servant of the Lord, the Lord said to Joshua, "Moses my servant is dead. Now then, you and all these people, get ready to cross the Jordan River into the land I am about to give to them—to the Israelites. I will give you every place where you set your foot, as I promised Moses. Your territory will extend from the desert to Lebanon, and from the great river, the Euphrates—all the Hittite country—to the Great Sea on the west" (Joshua 1:2–4, NIV).

This was the promise made to other people; now it's being made to the new generation. The old generation is gone. They are dead. Moses is dead, along with all the people who wouldn't cross the Jordan. They came to the edge of the Jordan, and

GOD said, "Across from this river is who you are. Across from this river is who I want you to be. The Semitic concept of land, Gan, is more than just a place that you occupy. The Semitic concept of land is who you are. The place that you inhabit is your identity" (see Deuteronomy 32:47).

So what GOD is really saying to the people of Israel is this: "You cross over into who you really are. The other side of the river is what I want you to do, who I want you to be, what I have called you to be. You have come from a very bad place, where your identity was really messed up. You have been told you are slaves. I want you to cross into a new land, a new identity. Everything that I have prepared for you, everything that I have made you to be, if you cross, it will all be yours."

And what did the old generation do? They sent twelve spies in, and they came back with gigantic grapes. Did you grow up with the Uncle Arthur *Bible Story* books? Remember the Maxwell books? With the two guys carrying the big old bunch of grapes the size of watermelons? Remember that? I used to stare at that stuff and think, *Wow, those are huge grapes. How would a person eat them?* And if those are big, imagine the ones in heaven. And if heaven has gigantic grapes like this, imagine what a mango would be like! I mean, watermelons would be the size of a church.

Anyway, the people of Israel probably looked at these gigantic grapes, thought about the size of the people who would eat those grapes, and heard the spies tell them, "No way; we'll be like roaches in there. I mean, they'll squash us up; it'll be disastrous. GOD isn't really meaning for us to cross there. You see, GOD has made it pretty comfortable here. We get manna every morning. We get that covering over the hot sun, keeps us nice and cool during the day. And then at night there is a nice pillar of light. This system works pretty good! Why would we cross over to the other side where there is danger? The other side is an enigma. It's unknown. GOD can't really mean to cross the Jordan. Because look at the size of the people!"

So the Israelites didn't. They went and walked around the wilderness for forty years, until everyone who did not believe that it could be done was gone.

Maybe GOD sometimes waits until those who don't believe are out of the way, and there is a new generation. This has nothing to do with age; it's about people who say it can't be done. You know, the people who say that the risks haven't been evaluated. They haven't called Risk Management to find out if this is approved by the board. It's the people who say, "We tried it before and it didn't work," or "The way we do it now works; why risk crossing?" The people who just hold back and sit on the banks of the Jordan and say, "It's comfy here, and I don't want to cross over because over there it is hard. I don't have a sleeping bag. I don't have a portable stove or my blow dryer. Over there it looks rough."

Life across the Jordan is what GOD wants for us. We should fear the day we get so complacent that we become the generation that has to die before GOD can do great things again. I have often wondered when that day will come for me. I think I might have reached it several times in the past couple of years.

Where There Is Faith

The other day a student walked into my office and said, "We are going to raise five thousand dollars for ADRA [Adventist Development and Relief Agency] here." This was during the tsunami-thing a few years ago. She said, "We are going to raise five thousand dollars from the students, *and* we are going to do it in one day."

I said, "That's sweet; that's so sweet. Jesus loves you so much."

I'm thinking, *You are going to try to extract five thousand dollars from students who are paying three million dollars to go to school every year? Good luck.*

She saw it. She read the doubt in my eyes and actually said to me, "What's wrong with you? You don't believe. You watch; you watch."

I said, "No, no, I believe. Go do it."

She said, "No, you don't!"

She walked out, and that day we raised twenty-thousand dollars! Not just five thousand. And guess who was humbled? Her . . . No, me.

My friends on Flower Street called me about a year and a half ago in the middle of the night, fired up because they heard a sermon I had preached on how I had served GOD. They asked me to come over. They live around the corner from me, so I ran over.

The guys on Flower Street are a bunch of bachelors living in a house together during their college years. Thumbs down on that, moms! Nutritionally bad . . .

hygienically bad . . . I go over there. They are so excited. They are giddy.

"What's going on?" I ask.

"Well, we've got this idea. We are going to get a boat—a ship, a big ship—like a fifty-passenger thing, and we are going to sail it from here all the way down to the South Pacific, and we are going to spend the rest of our lives just floating around all of Micronesia. All the South Pacific, all these islands, just serving people. And we'll have doctors and nurses, and all these people who will serve; and we'll build communities up, and we'll have teachers, and we'll build schools on every island. And we're just going to go there and minister to people."

"Wow! That's a really good idea."

I'm thinking, *If I go home right now, I can still get six hours of sleep.*

"We want you to come with us."

[Big sigh.] "Which one of you knows how to sail a ship?"

"What kind of question is that? Who cares? We'll figure it out. They have manuals at Barnes & Noble. We'll figure it out."

All these guys are on the edge of the Jordan. They see the other side; they know what GOD wants them to be. They are going to cross, right? They are ready to charge. And here I am on the comfortable side of the Jordan, thinking, *Oh brother, I have a mortgage payment. Is the ship going to cover that?*

I reply, "Have you noticed I have a wife and two kids?"

"They're coming too! We'll give them stuff to do on the boat."

"That's so sweet. Jesus loves you for having this vision."

Recently, one of those guys finished the process of forming a nonprofit organization and got the ship. And then it will be outfitted, and they are going to start sailing it. Who is part of the old generation that wouldn't cross? Check out http://mahi-intl.org/MAHI_International/Home.html, if you want to know more about their ministry.

Back to the Book

Wow, where were we? Back to Joshua. GOD says to the people, "Be the new generation. Be the people whom GOD calls to cross. Go across. Don't be the old people, the old generation that died in the wilderness. Don't say it can't be done. Don't say that isn't where GOD wants us."

Verse five. GOD says, "No one will be able to stand up against you all the days of your life. As I was with Moses, so I will be with you; I will never leave you nor forsake you" (NIV). If you are following along, verse six, prepare to jump: "Be strong and courageous" (NIV).

Verse seven: "Be strong and very courageous" (NIV).

Verse nine: "Have I not commanded you? Be strong and courageous. Do not be terrified; do not be discouraged, for the Lord your God will be with you wherever you go" (NIV).

I can hear GOD talking to me: "What is wrong with you? Do you believe? Of course we can raise five grand in one day. Be strong and courageous. You aren't going to accomplish anything for Me if you aren't strong and courageous. Yeah, it's going to take some courage to cross that river. You want to sit here the rest of your life or cross to where I really want you to be? It's going to take some courage."

Let's get to the actual crossing. Chapter three, verse eight. Something fascinating happens. "Tell the priests who carry the ark of the covenant: 'When you reach the edge of the Jordan's waters, go and stand in the river'" (NIV).

One day, while wrestling with this text, an archaeologist friend of mine said, "You know, Sam, what you have to understand is that during the time the Israelites were about to cross, during spring, most archaeologists and scholars believe the Jordan was at flood level, at flood stages. This is not like going to the beach." At flood stage, the Jordan is this massive current of water with steep, ten- to fifteen-foot drops in places, OK? So GOD says, "Step into the Jordan."

"As soon as the priests who carry the ark of the Lord—the Lord of all the earth—set foot in the Jordan, its water flowing downstream will be cut off and stand up in a heap" (verse 13, NIV). Here is a question I imagine Joshua was thinking: "Why don't You make the water stop first, GOD, and then we'll step in? Previously, You did this *shazzam* thing with the Red Sea. That was nifty. See, here is how it works. You're GOD—all powerful, all mighty. You go *whoooo*, and the water parts and then we cross. When it is safe, we cross. When it's good, when the life is obviously better for us than the one we have here, then we will cross. You first."

The rules change, though. From now on, as you read the Hebrew Bible, you see that the rules change for good. GOD says, "No, you first. From now on, you will see the power of GOD demonstrated when you believe, when you step into the water. Then you will see stuff happening. But if you sit on the bank of the Jordan, nothing will ever happen. Sure, I'll care for you; I'll take care of you. You'll get your manna; you'll get your little light, your little cloud.

"Cool. Nothing else will happen. But you will never be what I want you to be. Cross."

We try to make a deal with GOD and say, "You take care of my problems, and then I'll be a better person." This is how we pray. We get through the stuff about GOD really quick. "GOD, You are great, awesome. Love You. Now here is my list. Fix my wife, and then I will love her. Fix this relationship, do something to that person, and then I will fully give myself to him or her. Fix the quirks. They are so irritating. You fix my children. Make them behave, and then I will really be a good parent. GOD, You make me financially able to give more, and then I'll give more. You can't expect poor people to give, GOD. I have nothing. When You open up the storehouses of heaven, and You bless me with money, then You better believe that I will give.

"You stop the water, and then I will have more time for my church, the community, for my family, my kids, for everything You want me to have time for right now. But obviously, You can see that right now I don't have time, GOD. You help me believe, and then I will believe. You take away all these doubts I have about You, and then You watch—I'm going to be an amazing evangelist. I'm going to be Yours. You first, GOD."

My Own Jordan

You want to know what my Jordan is? I'll tell you. It's where I live. I've always seen it as this temporary thing. I'm not really from there. The other day in the paper, my neighborhood was called the methamphetamine capital of the world. No, we aren't the citrus capital. We aren't the "giant ball of yarn" capital. We are the methamphetamine capital of the world. Awesome.

A friend of mine walks into a wedding I was at last Sunday. He has gashes all over his head. Beaten up. Bruises everywhere. "John, what happened to you?"

"I got beat up. Next to the grocery store."

"Really, what were you doing?"

"I was carrying my groceries to the car."

Immediately this was my thinking: *Must get out of this place. Must get children away from this neighborhood. Not safe here.*

I was at a gas station. I had had a long day, a long Sabbath. Sabbath School, sermon for church, afternoon funeral, wedding rehearsal in the evening, and I'm heading home at nine or ten o'clock in the evening. I stop to get gas, and a young woman named Clarissa comes up to the car and says, "Can you spare a dollar for food?"

And I told her what I say to these people: "No, but if you are hungry, I'll give you one of my grocery cards that I carry right here in my glove compartment." But there were none there.

"I'll give you a granola bar, which I keep here for these occasions." Nothing there either.

So I asked, "What would you like?"

"Well, Taco Bell would be nice."

"OK, I'll get you Taco Bell."

"Well, can you get some for my husband, too, over there? His name is Jeff."

"OK, I'll get Jeff some Taco Bell. What would you like?"

Then Jeff goes, "If you are going to buy Taco Bell, would you buy Carl's Jr.?"

"What would you like?"

"The six-dollar burger."

"Well, that sounds pricey, Jeff."

"It's only four dollars." I don't understand that whole six-dollar burger for four dollars thing, but OK.

He says, "If you are willing to buy Carl's Jr., would you buy Denny's?"

"Jeff, it's your lucky night, because I'm feeling like maybe GOD wants me to cross this Jordan, and I'm going to sit with you, and we are going to have Denny's."

So we walked across to Denny's, and we sat down and started talking. I get really bold, which I never do, really, and ask where they are from.

"Colorado."

"What are you doing here?"

"It's cold in Colorado in the winter, so we come out here to Riverside."

"Why Riverside?"

"Because you can get drugs really easy here."

"Oh, really. Where do you get your drugs, exactly?"

"Five Points." He said it halfway through a bite.

Five Points—that's five blocks from where I live. I'm hoping it's not my Five Points, so I say to him, "Five Points where?"

So he describes the area. Yeah, that's the one. That's right where I live.

"So, it's really easy?"

"Yeah, that's why there's a lot of homeless people there. Everyone knows that if you want help, or drugs, that's where you go."

When they found out I'm a pastor, they told me they had been praying all day.

I said, "You've been praying all day? Because you are homeless, drug addicts, and you don't have your child with you? What's GOD doing for you, exactly?"

And Clarissa says to me, "We're eating, aren't we?"

They had been praying all day for food. Little steps, baby steps.

"Tomorrow we will pray for GOD to get us out of this addiction, and if that works, the next day we'll . . ."

What she's really saying is, "We're eating. Because you crossed."

Be Faithful and Courageous: Cross

I don't know what your Jordan is, but everyone has one. All of us have a river bank we are sitting on, and we are looking across to what GOD really wants us to do, to what He wants us to be, and we say, "Not right now, GOD. I'm comfortable here right now."

Some situations, some cycles that you just can't stop, some relationship that is just not working well, and you've always pointed over and said, "It's not my responsibility." And GOD is saying, "Yes, it's going to be scary, but you cross, and then you will see My power; then you will see what I can do."

GOD answers, "You want to see power, cross. Hand over this stuff. Surrender."

I was in the prayer room earlier, and in huge letters someone had written "Surrender." Surrender. Surrender to the leading of GOD and cross Jordan. This is what we are going to do.

What is the life that GOD wants for you, for me, for us? What is the life that GOD wants for me right now? What is the scary thing that you are looking at right now, that looks like what the Jordan had to have looked like to the people of Israel? What is that situation that looks scary? You know what it is. I know what mine is.

And with that in mind, meditate on these words:

"I will never leave you nor forsake you."

"Be strong and courageous."

"Have I not commanded you? Be strong and courageous. Do not be terrified; do not be discouraged, for the Lord your God will be with you wherever you go."[1]

Encounter

+ Describe your "Jordan." What would it look like for you to cross over?

4.3 You're an Angel

(Lynell LaMountain)

Forty-three-year-old Kerry Reardon was teaching his fifteen-year-old daughter how to drive. But she would learn more than how to guide a car through city traffic. She would learn how to be an angel.

The Howard Frankland Bridge was jammed with cars. Kerry told his daughter to get used to it because this happens all the time on the bridge. Then he saw skid marks, debris, and broken glass, but there was no car. He knew that a vehicle had flipped into the water.

Kerry had his daughter pull over. He got out of the car and looked over the edge. "I saw bubbles," he said. "Someone was still down there."

Mujo Jakupovic and his wife, Amira, had been driving east from St. Petersburg on the Howard Frankland at about 1:00 P.M. with their sons, thirteen-year-old Emrah and seven-year-old Amar. About two hundred yards from the end of the bridge, the left rear tire of their green 1998 Ford Explorer Sport blew out. "The car struck the inside wall," said Cpl. Jim Atwood of the Florida Highway

---

1. This entry is adapted from an article in the October 13, 2005 issue of the *Adventist Review*, which was originally adapted from a sermon given by Sam Leonor during GODencounters, May 27–June 4, 2004, in Apopka, Florida.

Patrol. "The car bounced across four lanes of traffic, rolling over before flipping over the side of the bridge."

The father, mother, and teenage son immediately escaped from the car. But the younger son was still inside. Tampa resident Kenny Hyatt saw the accident from his fishing boat and motored over to pick up the parents and teenage son. The car had plunged fourteen feet off the bridge and into nine feet of water. There was so much debris that Kenny couldn't see the car.

Kerry Reardon, a St. Petersburg native, used to dive off bridges as a young man to catch stone crabs. He saw that the current was swift, but he knew that if he dived deep enough he could avoid it. His daughter saw him dive headfirst into the murky water.

Reardon didn't find the car at first. He came up for air and went back down, where he found it, and seven-year-old Amar.

"He was just sitting there like a little rag doll," Reardon said. "I unbuckled him, pulled him out of the car and gave him his first breath of life."

As Reardon swam with the boy toward the fishing boat, a crowd was gathering on the bridge. Among them was Kelly Earle, twenty-five, a registered nurse from Bayfront Hospital, who was on her way to a baby shower for one of the physicians at Bayfront. Earle jumped into the water, knowing the child would probably need medical help. She swam to the fishing boat and began CPR. She doesn't really remember plunging into the water.

"It was pure adrenaline," said Earle, who works in Bayfront's obstetrics department. "I couldn't tell you what the temperature of the water was. It could have been fire for all I know."

Amar, dressed in his soccer clothes, was unconscious. His pulse was weak. As Earle continued CPR, Hyatt steered the boat toward shore, where an ambulance was waiting. The father and thirteen-year-old boy also needed medical attention.

Paramedics rushed them to Tampa General Hospital. The younger boy was in critical condition. Mujo Jakupovic and his older son were both in fair condition. The mother was unharmed.

Both Earle and Reardon were reluctant to claim any credit. Reardon said he just wanted people to pray for Amar. Earle said she'd feel better when the boy was home again with his family.

"Thankfully, everybody was in the right place," Earle said. "I just hope that it was enough."

Reardon's wife, Debbie, is certain that fate drew her husband to the crash. He had planned to spend his weekend competing in a kingfish tournament but withdrew at the last minute because he didn't catch enough bait. An act of bravery isn't out of character for him. In fact, the family teasingly calls him "Rambo."

"Someone definitely put him there," said Debbie Reardon. "He was meant to be somebody's angel."

And so are you. You are meant to be somebody's angel.

To somebody who is hurting or helpless, whether it's giving them a cup of water, holding them while they cry, or listening to their silly knock-knock jokes, you've been commissioned to be an angel, their angel, to breathe into them the breath of GOD and ignite their soul's life and joy.

Spread your wings and fly (or dive). You're an angel of hope.

Encounter the Word

After reading Matthew 25:31–46, give special attention and meditation to the following passage:

"The King will reply, 'I tell you the truth, whatever you did for one of the least of these brothers of mine, you did for me'" (Matthew 25:40, NIV).

Encounter

- Who in your life might need some encouragement or hope? What authentic actions can you take to support them?
- Who are the "least of these" people in your life? What draws you or repels you about them?
- Beyond the extraordinary events (mission trips, life-saving rescues), what ordinary, everyday things could you do to be a hero of hope?

4.4 GOD Is Where?

(Todd Gable)

While taking forensic psychology, I had the opportunity to visit a prison. I looked on the outing with mixed feelings. I really didn't know what to expect, but if you watch enough movies and TV and hear enough stories, you can understand why I was a little apprehensive.

For several weeks, I had secretly rejoiced that we weren't going because something came up or the trip was rescheduled, or whatever other difficulty popped up. Outwardly, I was disappointed, but inwardly, well, I wasn't losing any sleep over it. When the call came and I knew that we were going, I was a little nervous and holding on to a dim hope that something would come up once again.

It would seem, however, that GOD is not without a sense of humor. We got to the prison and were asked to sign in. *So far so good*, I was thinking. Then we were frisked, which actually made a great deal of sense to me. One of my fellow classmates, Paul, had to leave his coffee mug in the car, the poor guy. I've never seen anyone drink coffee that fast before, and it couldn't have been that much fun. Everyone else made it in without incident, though. I did, however, stay near Jonathan and Donny, who are both a little taller than me.

The chaplain was giving us a tour of the place, and we began by walking through the women's ward. I'll not bore you with the mundane details. We got to see many different aspects of the prison, and then we ended up in the men's library, which was also where the chaplain's office was.

Two inmates agreed to come in and speak with us. We were able to ask them why they were there and basically anything else we could think of, but they were under no obligation to tell us anything. The more talkative of the two had quite a few things to say, and I was amazed at what I was hearing.

He was a black man in his midforties, and he was in for his second six-month sentence for minor theft. He said that he had children, and that drugs were the actual reason he was there. He told us that he used to deal and do drugs, and that cocaine was his drug of choice. He discussed being an addict, and how even if you manage to break away from your drug of choice, just doing something else like having some alcohol will undoubtedly lead you right back to it. His oldest son was in a federal penitentiary, he informed us, and he blamed himself for it because he always had drugs in the house when the boy was younger.

He proceeded then to say something that rocked my world. He informed us rather boldly that we need to take time and associate with our children, and that the family that prays together stays together. That, from a man who was in prison!

It really got me to thinking about how GOD is in the most bizarre places. I was loathing having to go to this prison, thinking that all the inmates there really deserved what they got. I had a low opinion of the place before I even set foot there. But GOD, in His infinite wisdom, put me exactly where I needed to be.

It reminds me of a verse I read in Romans, which says, "Oh, the depth of the riches both of the wisdom and knowledge of God! How unsearchable are His judgments and unfathomable His ways!" (Romans 11:33, NASB). What Paul is saying to me is that GOD already knows more than I do because He's been here longer and He is Creator of all things. I didn't want to go to the prison because I thought I knew what was there, but GOD showed me that I didn't know anything about it, and that He had already been in that place. It was very humbling. Of all the places where I expected to find GOD, I found Him where? I found my Jesus in a prisoner, and it was exactly when I needed Him, even if I didn't know it.

When you face trials in life, always remember that GOD is there and always has been, and He will get you through.

Encounter the Word

"As a prisoner for the Lord, then, I urge you to live a life worthy of the calling you have received. Be completely humble and gentle; be patient, bearing with one another in love. Make every effort to keep the unity of the Spirit through the bond of peace" (Ephesians 4:1–3, NIV).

Encounter

+ What is the most unlikely place where you learned something about GOD?
+ Find the lowly places in your life. How have you encountered GOD there?
+ No matter our life circumstance, status, or vocation, we are given opportunities to be GOD's emissary. What ways will you foster GODencounters for those you intersect with today?

4.45 Per Diem Work, Full-Time Stress

(Shayna Bailey)

"I love Mission Manor!" she happily declared.

With the extra emphasis on *love*, A. D. squirmed with delight in her chair.

We were sitting in one of the group therapy rooms of the Adolescent Girls Inpatient Unit. With her feet perched on her chair in front of her, A. D. contorted her body and tugged at the Velcro pulls on her open blue hospital gown. She was wearing it over her jeans and T-shirt.

"What's Mission Manor?" I prodded.

"It's a drug rehab program," she informed me. "They have the best food! I've been there five times already," she bragged.

I hadn't read A. D.'s chart yet, so I didn't know her official diagnosis. In group, however, she was being candid with certain revelations about her past.

"I'm a rebel," she told the group. "I love breaking the law and getting caught. But I'll stop. Before I'm seventeen. You know, it doesn't count when you're a minor."

"Do you think that's the right attitude for you to have, A. D.?" I interjected. "You know that we expect you to learn better coping mechanisms when you're here. What if you can't stop?"

She feigned remorse. "I know. I was just joking."

It was obvious that A. D. knew the routine of psychotherapy groups. She knew the right things to say at the right times. With the group needing to continue, though, I didn't have any more time for what the unit nurses called "war stories." I refocused with a simple comment.

"Come and find me this afternoon. I want to talk to you more."

I didn't expect A. D. to take me up on my offer. I mean, who was I? It was my first inpatient day, and it was painfully obvious that I was merely an outpatient mental healthcare worker who didn't really know what she was doing. Truth be told, I was concerned that A. D. might have thought I was mocking her when I broke my language down to ghetto-fabulous street terminology. I do it all the time with the outpatients, but I could see how a seasoned psychiatric patient would be skeptical.

Around 2:00 P.M., my coworker Frank was engrossed in telling me stories about his humanitarian work with MADD. While he rambled into my left ear, I kept a watchful eye on the girls in the common room while they had their afternoon snack. I was distracted by the nurses bustling around me and the obligatory nod I was making at Frank every few seconds. I didn't think much of it when A. D. appeared in front of me at the nurses' station.

"Stay in the common room while you're eating," a nurse instructed her.

Two minutes later, she was back.

"Did you hear me?" the nurse asked. "In the common room, please!"

I don't know that I even acknowledged A. D.'s presence. I might have smiled before glancing at the clock and willing it in vain for it to reach 3:00 P.M., the end of my shift. Then it was back to watching the girls, especially those on "close observation."

Two hours later, I was lying in bed. Like I've had to do every day this week, I had closed my bedroom door, drawn my curtains shut, and then climbed beneath my comforter. Lying in silence in the middle of the afternoon, I was processing the talking faces disclosing abuse, neglect, rape, incest, psychosis, delusions, hallucinations, family history, and environmental stressors.

It was during this time that I remembered A. D.'s appearance.

There had been so many people to watch, so many charts to remember, and so much fear about the one psychotic girl on the unit that the other staff had entreated me to avoid. I felt incompetent and overtired and that I had not made the effort I usually make with outpatients. If I had, I would have remembered to find A. D. myself—even if she hadn't wanted to talk to me.

I know that the only way to learn is with experience, but because of my self-doubt and distraction, I overlooked A. D. the same way that people probably have all of her life. I guess there will always be understaffed hospitals, staff members who don't pay attention, and patients who don't receive adequate treatment. But there will also be another shift and the opportunity to try one more time.

Encounter the Word

"When he saw the crowds, he had compassion on them, because they were harassed and helpless, like sheep without a shepherd" (Matthew 9:36, NIV).

Encounter

+ What simple, ordinary gestures might be welcomed by a neglected someone who crosses your path regularly?
+ What helps you be sensitive to the GODencounters to be found in your

everyday workplace, classroom, or campus?

+ How can you express who Jesus is to the "overlooked"?

4.5 Heard About Pixie?

(Lynell LaMountain)

The house was filled with smoke and flames.

Firefighters dashed inside and rescued everyone, including Pixie, a twelve-pound terrier crossbreed.

There were no injuries except for Pixie's. She was having a seizure. Her back was arched, and her mouth was wide open. She wasn't breathing.

Firefighter LeBlanc took Pixie, put his mouth on the dog's mouth, and tried to revive her. Another firefighter gave her oxygen. Then they rushed Pixie to a veterinary clinic for emergency treatment.

The dog, owned by Phil and Kathy Kindler, survived.

"She's looking good and breathing comfortably," veterinarian Dr. Elizabeth Brandt told *The Salem News*.[2]

Captain Alan Dionne commented that the firefighters' work exemplifies an important ethical guideline in the firefighting profession: "Save lives first, property second. It's always life first. And that means every life."

I love that guideline.

We live in an age when our respect for "life" doesn't seem as sacred as it once was. Every week we see awful stories of painful acts. And we read news stories about political debates regarding our government's use (or not) of human torture. Nearly every day we see lives exploited for profit. Not to mention the exploitation of our natural resources, and our seemingly total disinterest in animals unless they're a menu item.

So, I love this story about firefighter LeBlanc, and Captain Dionne's statement: "It's always life first. . . . And that means every life."

That's a motto we should all adopt, because it's an expression of love and a respectful acknowledgment of what's most sacred. It's also a reflection of our

---

2. Officials think faulty wiring caused the fire. Here's a link to the story: http://firstcoastnews .com/news/strange/news-article.aspx?storyid=48906.

Creator's heart. "With long life will I satisfy him and show him my salvation" (Psalm 91:16, NIV).

Today and tomorrow, go out of your way to do something special—something intentional that requires thought and energy on your part, and that demonstrates your support, respect, and gratitude for life. All life.

Encounter the Word

"So God created man in his own image, in the image of God he created him; male and female he created them. God blessed them and said to them, 'Be fruitful and increase in number; fill the earth and subdue it. Rule over the fish of the sea and the birds of the air and over every living creature that moves on the ground' " (Genesis 1:27, 28, NIV).

Encounter

+ How do you express your compassion other than to people?
+ In what ways does your authority over the earth (animals, plant life, environment) exhibit the grace of GOD?
+ What can you begin to do today that will exhibit a grace-filled respect for life, all life?

4.6 "Wouldn't GOD Want You To?"

(Shayna Bailey)

I was still dazed and anxious from the stress of almost missing my flight. I was praying that my luggage would make it onto my flight to L.A., but even if it didn't, I was grateful that I would. Stepping onto the plane, I saw that in the third row, an elderly woman was sitting in the window seat.

"Is anyone sitting here?" I asked, pointing to the aisle seat in her row. I had grown accustomed to asking the question on Southwest Airlines.

"No, you can sit here," she said pleasantly.

As I plopped down, I was elated at having secured an aisle seat—my mission of the day. Even better, I was sitting with a nice old lady instead of an obese football player (you'd be surprised how many times this has happened) encroaching into my small space of seat and actually thinking he's entitled to my arm rest.

As more passengers joined the flight, a twenty-something woman carrying a backpack asked for the middle seat. I got up, and she slid in.

Elderly Lady was pleased that she had landed two young, friendly passengers to share her row with. She wasted no time initiating conversation.

"What do you do for a living?" she asked the woman sitting next to me. "And do you like it? How long have you been doing it?"

The questions were flowing at a rapid pace, and I was grateful that the woman next to me was the subject of Elderly Lady's interrogation. While she chatted it up, I could concentrate on working without feeling guilty or rude. I pulled out my laptop and shoved my iPod earbuds in. This was going to be a noninterrupted business flight for me, if I could help it.

Unfortunately, I couldn't help it.

When Elderly Lady had tired our other companion, she leaned forward in her seat to direct her conversation to me. I pulled an earbud free, listening and smiling about her passion to save the planet and her mission to write a book exposing the travesties of the O. J. Simpson case.

"One attorney said that the case showed that murder is now legal in our country," she said. "Can you imagine that? I'm going to write a book about it."

Elderly Lady was well-intentioned, and I really didn't mind talking to her at all. I knew she was relishing the attention she was getting from her two row mates. After three hours, though, the endless talking became too much. I noticed that, in between naps, the woman next to me also put her iPod earbuds in—the universal sign for "I don't want to talk to you." To get our attention, Elderly Lady had to resort to either screaming above the noise of our iPods or tapping one of our legs.

There was the direction to look at what she was eating for lunch. And did you know that the Sierra Club has five tips each month on how to conserve? Look at the Rocky Mountains.

"Wow, they're beautiful." I elevated my voice in response to the last instruction. "Thank you for letting me know we are flying over them."

When we passed over the Grand Canyon an hour later, a small huddle of people from the other side of the aircraft appeared in the aisle next to me. They were leaning and craning over me and the woman next to me (apparently the Grand Canyon is more interesting than the Rocky Mountains), so I didn't think it was necessary for Elderly Lady to instruct us to look out the window. There were already six people vying for a glimpse.

"Look! The Grand Canyon!" she said.

The woman next to me turned to the window, but I was midsentence in my typing and not really interested. Elderly Lady quickly became agitated with me and said, almost pleadingly, "Why didn't you look? Wouldn't *GOD* want you to?"

The woman next to me stifled a laugh.

Elderly Lady knew that I was a Christian writer, and I'm sure her comment was at least partly related to this fact.

"GOD would definitely want me to look," I answered.

"Well, it's almost gone!" she said frantically.

"It's OK," I assured her. "I've visited the Grand Canyon before. But, thank you."

She seemed assured, but slightly embarrassed at her tantrum, so I smiled and listened to her talk about global warming for another five minutes.

I've heard a lot of justifications for what GOD would want us to do. *GOD* told me you are "the one." GOD told me that you aren't. GOD told me I should talk to you about how your behavior is a stumbling block. Rarely, if ever, do I ever hear meaningful elaborations on what GOD would really want us to do, though. GOD would want me to encourage you, instead of judging you. GOD would want me to apologize and ask forgiveness. GOD would want me to listen more than I talk.

The one thing that has been terrifying me about my job lately is the prospect of being able to interpret GOD's Word effectively for people. Deuteronomy 4:2 warns us, "Do not add to what I command you and do not subtract from it, but keep the commands of the Lord your God that I give to you" (NIV). I've been plagued with insecurity about whether I am misinterpreting the Bible in the columns that I write, and now, the sermons that I am preaching. Do I really get the messages in the way that GOD intends for me to? Who am I to tell someone else what the Bible says?

Yet, here I am in So Cal for ten days—preaching at the largest Seventh-day Adventist churches in the country. As far as what GOD would want me to do, well, I'm trying my best to deliver clear and effective messages. And, to represent

77

Him in what I do and who I am. I think that more than anything, that's all GOD wants any of us to do.

Encounter the Word

"The Lord has shown you what is good. He has told you what he requires of you. You must treat people fairly. You must love others faithfully. And you must be very careful to live the way your God wants you to" (Micah 6:8, NIrV).

Encounter

+ What message about GOD does your life convey? How do people perceive GOD in their interaction with you?
+ How is your faith expressed in how you pursue your career?
+ Even if you are not in ministry as a profession, what message of grace do you aspire to relate in your workplace or on your campus?

4.7 Meet Dejie

(Lynell LaMountain)

They won't see their seven-year-old son, Dejie, grow up, because they don't have enough money for his medicine. Dejie is in the leukemia unit of Beijing Children's Hospital. And doctors have warned his parents that as soon as their money dries up, so will the medicine . . . and their hope.[3]

China has what's called a pay-as-you-go health system: cash up front, or no treatment. The World Health Organization ranked China fourth from the bottom in terms of the fairness of its health coverage, in a survey issued in 2000.

Dejie's mom, Yang Deyin, traveled more than three hundred miles by bus to Beijing from their small farm in Mongolia to be near her only child. She camped out on a blue plastic chair in the hospital waiting room to save money on lodging.

Back home, her husband asked relatives and village neighbors for more loans to secure Dejie's continued treatment. If you watched Yang most nights, you would see her checking the hospital's computers to see how much cash remained in their hospital-controlled account. Sometimes the number flashed red, meaning that they were behind. So she'd call her husband and plead with him to find more money for Dejie.

---

3. Dejie's story can be found on the front page of the *Wall Street Journal*, December 5, 2005.

In the past few weeks, this mother and father have begun realizing that they won't be seeing their son grow up. His leukemia is considered highly treatable, but, at present, they're unable to raise the $18,500 to complete his six-month course of treatment. That amount doesn't sound like much to save a child. But when you make less than $350 per year, as Dejie's parents do, $18,500 is more than sixty years of wages.

Dejie's dad has already dug up their potato crop and sold it all. He has threshed the corn and sold almost all of that, too. There's nothing left to sell, and no more money to be borrowed. Looking out across his farm, he slumps in the doorway of his house and sighs. "I'll just have to fetch Dejie home to die."

How awful.

From this I get a clearer understanding of the text that says of Abraham, "By faith he made his home in the promised land like a stranger in a foreign country; he lived in tents . . . for he was looking forward to the city with foundations, whose architect and builder is God" (Hebrews 11:9, 10, NIV). While we live to make this world a better place by demonstrating goodwill toward all people, we must always remember that we are foreigners on this earth, because our citizenship is in another country and our residence is in another city—a city built by GOD.[4] A city without hospitals and tears. A city where families never have to say Goodbye. A city where we can enjoy our loved ones forever. A city where every story has a happy ending.

Seems there's always tension between content and discontent. On the one hand, I'm content with my life and GOD's manifested will. On the other hand, I'm profoundly discontented that I'm still here in this "foreign" land.

We should do everything in our power to not allow our hearts to be attached to this world.

How?

1. Enjoy conversation with GOD daily.

2. Enjoy serving humanity in some way regularly.

3. Pray for GOD to advance His love *in* you and *through* you.

4. Pray for all the Dejies of the world right now, and let GOD develop within

---

4. You can read more about our city in Revelation 21.

you an active faith that demonstrates hope to a dying world.

Encounter the Word

After reading Luke 10:25–37, give special attention and meditation to the following passage:

" 'Love the Lord your God with all your heart and with all your soul and with all your strength and with all your mind'; and, 'Love your neighbor as yourself.' 'You have answered correctly,' Jesus replied. 'Do this and you will live' " (Luke 10:27, 28, NIV).

Encounter

+ How can you begin to establish heaven here on earth? What ways do you exhibit the new kingdom values in the midst of the travesty of the current conditions?
+ In what ways do you enjoy serving humanity regularly?
+ How is GOD impressing you to express love your for "neighbors" beyond the ones next door?

4.8 Entertaining Angels

(Shayna Bailey)

Lately I've been talking to strangers.

Now before you start the lecture on safety and common sense, my parents gave me the same speeches yours did. Rest assured that I've been locking my car doors and staying in well-lit public areas, in spite of my recent compulsion.

Usually the stranger is alone, like I am, in a very nonsketchy place—a restaurant, Internet café, or airport terminal. Conversation begins and ends in the name of short-lived companionship and nothing more.

A few weeks ago in Washington-Dulles International airport, a woman wearing black and white introduced me to her very colorful past. While we waited for the Terminal B shuttle, she revealed saucy details about two divorces, a shameful and scandalous teenage pregnancy in a well-to-do family, and her purpose in traveling that morning—to reconcile things with ex-husband number two, "a tan, skinny Frenchman living in Palm Beach."

She learned of my profession, my views about dating and marriage, and the angst I was experiencing about a new guy in my own love life. The conversation scarcely lasted ten minutes before we parted and proceeded to our respective gates without even stating our names.

Intimate banter for strangers in an airport, don't you think?

I thought about the comments made in a few minutes for a few days, though, and even rented and watched a movie that this stranger told me was a must-see. Clearly her words had a far-reaching impact.

It's true that anonymity prompts us to talk about our darkest secrets, knowing that we will never see our conversation mates again. This particular stranger had to be nervous about that reconciliation conversation that would be happening when she landed. I was there, she was there . . . hey, why not talk about it?

Hebrews 13:2 entreats us, though, "Do not forget to entertain strangers, for by so doing some people have entertained angels without knowing it" (NIV). More plainly stated: *Chance meetings aren't always by chance.*

Have you ever had someone walk up to you and say exactly what you needed to hear, right when you needed to hear it? Has anyone ever told you that you were that person for them?

Tell us about it.

Encounter

+ What "chance" encounters have turned out to be providential for you?
+ What will help you be more keenly aware of GODencounters that daily come your way?
+ How might you entertain these interactions in a way that gracefully expresses your love for GOD?

My Experience

_____

_____

_____

_____

5.0 PRAYER

5.1 Pray Without Ceasing

It is our desire to experience the presence and power of the living GOD through a life of prayer. We're learning to seek deep intimacy with GOD continually, without ceasing. Prayer and meditation shape our lifestyle.

5.15 Unstoppable Vow

(Whitni Roche)

I vow
to light the fire of prayer
in my life daily.
Throughout this next year,
I choose
to enter into the stillness
of GOD's presence,
abiding in Him.
I will wait
in eager expectation
for the Spirit to move
in this world in response
to my fervent,
unstoppable prayer.

5.2 Breathe

(Lynell LaMountain)

Ever held your breath until you were so desperate for air that your toes twitched, your cheeks became balloons, and your eyes bugged out? Overpowered by deprivation, did you sip air in all properlike, or did you swig down big gulps like a scorched vagabond at a thirst-quenching oasis?

Our lungs crave air. Our soul craves GOD—fresh, life-giving . . . GOD. We ache for an encounter with Him. Do you know what it feels like to yearn for, long for, to covet GOD?

I drove into Camp Kulaqua just outside of High Springs, Florida, for the GODencounters Retreat. I had been asked to teach a seminar on prayer. Although I had taught many times on the subject of prayer, I didn't know what to expect from this "GODencounters" thing. Being a movie buff, all I could picture was Spielberg's *Close Encounters* with flashing UFO lights.

Friday night began with curriculum coach Allan Martin's preface: "If you've come here to be entertained, you've come to the wrong place. We're not here to entertain you or make you feel good. We're not offering you a showy religious program. We're here because of a *sacred discontent*. We're here to encounter GOD because we're dissatisfied with what was good enough before. We want to live in His presence twenty-four-seven."

The room was still—the kind of stillness you feel before an approaching storm. As the reality of the statement settled into people's minds, the storm came. There was a cacophony of unsolicited amens and applause. Worship started, and hundreds of young adults shook GOD's house with their breaths of praise. Deep breaths. Long breaths. Cherished breaths. Eternal breaths.

The meeting may have ended, but worship continued into the night in various prayers rooms, including an A-frame lodge that had been transformed into a living prayer sanctuary, with ten interactive prayer stations guiding you in your holy encounter with your Father. Tea lights and scented candles flickered throughout the room, as soft music added to the warm ambiance.

The first thing I saw was a sign: "Take off your shoes because you are standing on holy ground." So I did. And then I inhaled—not the proper, image-conscious

breaths I take at religious programs, but deep breaths—filling up on GOD's crisp, energizing presence.

I was in a mall not long ago and passed by an *oxygen bar*. People sat on stools along a counter that was topped with shampoo-sized cylinders bubbling with different colors of liquid—yellow, green, red, blue. Maybe you've seen them. Covering the nose and mouth of each customer was a mask. Attached to the mask was a tube. Being piped through the tube was crisp oxygen. It's called the "oxygen experience," and it promises to "pick you up" and energize you.

At the GODencounters Retreat, I experienced how Elijah must have felt when GOD told him, "Go out and stand on the mountain in the presence of the LORD, for the LORD is about to pass by" (1 Kings 19:11, NIV). I knew I was in the presence of GOD. Hallelujah! And I didn't want to leave. I yearned to remain within this Oxygen Experience—I coveted it, because the breath of GOD was reviving my soul.

My soul was not alone; others were being revived too. Covering the prayer room wallpaper were etchings in crayon, markers, and pen. Scribbles and sentences from other breathtaking souls.

"[I give You] My life, totally. My weakness, my fears."

"Lord, please allow my family and I to see You face to face in the clouds of glory and to hear You say, 'Well done thou good and faithful servant.' "

"May I worship You forever! Your praises are my life!"

"I offer my life to You. Take control of it and lead me to You. Let my vision be Jesus."

"Dear GOD, I'm sorry for leaving You. I miss your presence and I want to be with You and You with me . . . please be present again in my life. I'm coming back to You. Help me. Your child."

His children breathe in His presence. The speaker, the worship leader, and the music-facilitated worship endorsed our royal relationship with GOD as His sons and daughters. Practical seminars, creative communion, and anointing services refreshed our practice of being in His presence. Just being with hundreds of other young-adult GODfollowers through the weekend—at praise, at play, at prayer, at peace—was CPR for the soul.

Sebastian Zaldibar, a twenty-eight-year-old social work major, concurred.

"Throughout the entire weekend, I felt the Spirit tugging constantly at my heart and impressing upon me to realize who I am, that I am a son of GOD. That fact completely changed my perspective on myself and how I view others around me . . . The most important aspect of GODencounters was understanding who I am, realizing that the only way to go to GOD in complete surrender is to know who I am and *who* I need in my life."

"[At GODencounters] I finally accepted Jesus personally," said Rebecca Sarah Ali of Miami, Florida. "I learned that GOD is my Dad. I can actually develop a relationship with Him . . . a relationship full of truth—no secrets—and He will literally forgive me and hold nothing against me!"

Biology major Christina Jimenez shared the impact of GODencounters. "I got to see a lot of people cry out to GOD for love and peace in their lives . . . It impacted my relationship with Jesus in a very good way."

"I was prayed over . . . and felt the power of the Holy Spirit . . . like I was dancing with Jesus, I just stayed in silence—enjoying this time—and had a conversation with Him," recalled Nicki Carleton, a thirty-one-year-old missionary from Australia. "It was so nice, like getting a beautiful hug."

To ache for GOD's presence. To desire His embrace 24/7. To have our souls oxygenated with the Holy Spirit! To simply fall into the arms of grace when your soul is too weary to stand, and be carried for a few steps on your journey home. To live like you are His child. Oxygen for the soul—this is GODencounters.

"This is what the Sovereign Lord says to these bones: I will make breath enter you, and you will come to life."

Breathe.

Encounter the Word

"This is what the Sovereign Lord says to these bones: I will make breath enter you, and you will come to life" (Ezekiel 37:5, NIV).

Encounter

+ Feeling out of breath? What do you wish to exhale from your life? What characteristics of GOD do you wish to inhale?
+ Has superficial chatting kept you from really sharing with GOD what's on your mind? What's on your mind? Listen to His response.

5.25 What Women (Really) Want

(Shayna Bailey)

It was gray and raining when the nurse called me last fall. I had flippantly written about the office visit preceding this call, but I wouldn't have if I had known what was coming next.

"We have your lab work back," she announced. "Can you hold while I get the doctor?" From that moment on, I knew that there was bad news. They never have the doctor talk to you. Usually, you just get a two-second call from a nurse. Otherwise, you receive a delightfully impersonal lab sheet in the mail a few weeks later. They only ask you to wait for the doctor when something's terribly wrong.

I was shaking by the time Dr. P.'s voice greeted me on the other line.

"Unfortunately," she started, "you've tested positive for lupus."

As I sat trembling and horrified on the couch, I missed most of what Dr. P. said next. She mentioned "false positives," "don't worry," "symptom control," and "you're young." Then she ended with, "You need to come back whenever you're having symptoms. We'll retest in a year."

I don't know how long I sat breathless and shaking before I called David. Interrupting his work day, I squeaked out a feeble, "Can you come home?"

I waited for him to arrive. I wanted him to tell me that everything would be fine. That he would help me face this. That I shouldn't worry. And when he arrived an hour later, he did. I listened without believing, though, and sobbed warm tears into his dress shirt.

Eventually, his propensity to be rational and lucid surfaced. "You have to be proactive about this," he advised me.

Proactive was the very opposite of what I wanted to be, though. I would visit WebMD almost daily, only to terrify myself and close the Web pages immediately. During routine visits with Dr. P., I would downplay my symptoms and deny the overwhelming lethargy and depression that was stifling me. For months, I vacillated between happiness that the symptoms weren't in my head and terror that everything I wanted out of life was being invalidated by the lack of physical health I needed to accomplish them.

Unable to wrap my brain around the tragedy of starting life as a twenty-three-year-old lupus patient, I adopted the worst possible mantra for my own health: out of sight, out of mind.

Eventually, though, that changed.

I decided that it was worthless to psych myself out of all the good things that GOD had planned for me. I realized that it was futile to depend on another person to give me hope about my own health. I claimed the promises of health and survival, even through challenges. Then, I made an appointment with a new doctor.

Earlier this month, I sat bravely in her office. Providing a lengthy description of my medical history, I said the words that have held me captive to fear for the past year.

"Last fall I screened positive for lupus. I was told that I needed to have myself checked again. I'd like to do that today."

Without letting anyone know that I had scheduled this appointment, I sat quietly and alone while my blood was drawn. I knew that there would be no David to run to afterwards this time. But for the first time in a long time, I was confident that I could get through this.

So when the mailing from Johns Hopkins Community Physicians arrived the day before I left for California, I expected a bill or insurance report. Instead, a completely delightful and impersonal lab report slid out. On it, my doctor has scrawled a note before her signature, "Test was negative."

Encounter the Word

"Answer me when I call to you, O my righteous God. Give me relief from my distress; be merciful to me and hear my prayer" (Psalm 4:1, NIV).

Encounter

+ Where in your life is there uncertainty? Who do you go to for help?
+ When you pray to GOD, what do you hope will happen? What impact does conversing with Him have on your confidence?
+ What is GOD's reaction to your worst-case scenarios? When is your prayer life most active?

5.3 Showing Up

(Erika Larson-Hueneke)

It was 5:00 A.M. on March 27, 2004. I was driving. The highway was empty, and Central Florida was sleeping. When I got to my destination, I wrote in my journal, "The sun rises over west Orlando. The sky lightens behind the backdrop of a sprinkle of skyscrapers as I speed to the prayer room at Church in the Son. Lord, help me to see not buildings but lives, not lights but souls."

The 24/7 prayer room had officially opened the night before. The idea was to have people praying twenty-four hours a day, seven days a week, each person taking a one-hour shift in a small room, with prayers and drawings scratched on the walls. I scheduled my inaugural shift for sunrise, and it would be the first time I would ever spend that much time in concentrated prayer, although I had "accepted Jesus" when I was only four years old.

Over the next several months, I would repeatedly make the half-hour trip to that room, at varying times of the day, and it would literally change my life. I would watch healing unfold before my very eyes, as someone close to me truly mourned for the first time over sexual abuse they had experienced in the past. I would hear the account of an all-night vigil held for a young man trapped in addiction and debt, and of that man choosing to seek freedom by returning to his family, like a modern-day prodigal son. I would sit in the room in the middle of the night, GOD's presence thick around me like it might have been as Moses stood beside the burning bush.

But I didn't yet know that those things would come to pass when I sleepily drove to the prayer room that first night. I couldn't know what was ahead as I pleaded with GOD in my journal—"HEAL Your people. Bring us forgiveness for each other. Bring us respect. Honor. Patience. Intimacy in Your Spirit. Pure thoughts. Pure words. Beautiful agape love. *Purge* insecurity from our lives. Replace it with utter confidence in Your Spirit. Give us boldness to face our pasts, initiate the hard conversations, be open and obedient to Your leading."

I couldn't know then what amazing things GOD would go on to do in those months. But I had to be faithful to show up anyway.

Encounter the Word

"Very early in the morning, while it was still dark, Jesus got up, left the house and went off to a solitary place, where he prayed" (Mark 1:35, NIV).

Encounter

+ Where is GOD asking you to show up? Will you do it, even if it requires some kind of sacrifice?
+ Do you believe that as you are faithful to do what He asks, He will be faithful to do the redeeming work?
+ What have you asked of GOD? What have you sensed He asks of you?

5.35 Prayer Optimization

(Lynell LaMountain)

You take your car in for tune-ups. You defrag your computer's hard drive. You optimize your software permissions. But sometimes our prayers need maintenance too. Here are three steps to optimize your prayer life:

1. Be consistent.

Persistence and consistency are the twin powers of success. Is your prayer life streaky? One month it's an arid desert experience, the next it's an invigorating oasis of communion with GOD.

2. Be sincere.

Praying prayers from a book, or praying them out of duty (blessing your food before eating it, for example), are, well, uninspiring. What's going on in your life today? Your life, not your duty, is the backbone of durable (and doable, I might add) prayer.

3. Be honest.

Sometimes we wonder if praying will make a difference. Be honest with GOD about this. If He knows everything, why should I pray about this? Be honest. If He knows everything (and He does), then He knows how you feel. Be honest. Because you can't offend Him or push Him away. GOD doesn't hold grudges. He doesn't love you for what you do pray or for what you don't pray; He just loves you.

The power of prayer doesn't reside in the one who prays it, but in the One who hears it.

Encounter the Word

After reading all of chapter 14 of John, give special attention and meditation to the following passage:

"And I will do whatever you ask in my name, so that the Son may bring glory to the Father. You may ask me for anything in my name, and I will do it" (John 14:13, 14, NIV).

Encounter

+ Who do you feel like you can tell anything to? What characteristics of the human relationship apply to prayer life?
+ What reaction might you imagine GOD having to your prayers?
+ What intrudes or interrupts your prayer life? What steps can you take to prevent this?

5.4 On Letting Go

(Shayna Bailey)

I felt a grin creeping across my face as Sessa handed me the mail. There, on top, was a letter from David.

"I can't believe this got here already," I commented to Sessa. "I just told his secretary *yesterday* where to mail it."

David could have sent this online, but I surmised that he had chosen to mail it with ulterior motives. The last time we had talked, I mentioned that Sessa and I were moving. By mailing the envelope, David's secretary would have to solicit a current address from me.

Our last conversation was in November. Sessa and I had just returned from Thanksgiving, and with us both being out of town for several days, we decided to leave a key to the apartment with David. It wasn't an ideal decision, but because he was a trusted mutual friend who wouldn't mind the menial task of watering the plants and feeding the fish, we had asked him. And, he had come.

Several nights later, he had driven down to the city to return the spare key to us. His twenty-seventh birthday had just passed, so as he stood in our illuminated foyer, I asked him what he wanted. I still cared about him deeply, and we were obviously on friendly terms. But, having dinner would be too romantic and possibly suggest the desire for reconciliation. The original plan of throwing David a surprise birthday party had to be voided too. What does a recently broken-up ex-girlfriend give to her ex-boyfriend?

I offered him the aquarium. "I was going to put a few really nice exotic fish in it," I told him. "I think it would look great in your house." After all, tropical fish are basically synonymous with bachelor pads. David was the one who had bestowed the aquarium on me in the first place. Returning the once-empty container in a jazzed-up, trendier form seemed thoughtful and fitting. I didn't think he would say No. But he did.

He handed me the keys and told me he would "think of something." And he left.

A few minutes later, my cell phone rang.

"I thought of something," he said. "Remember the Rosetta Stone Hindi software I bought you? I want that back."

I don't think he meant it to sound like we were having a post-split division of assets, so he quickly followed up with, "Well, I mean, if you're not using it, of course. You're not using it, are you?" he asked.

"I am, actually," I confidently informed him. "I'm learning it to spite your parents." The words escaped before I had time to consider their implications. What I had said was true, but I shouldn't have said it. Proverbs 18:21 tells us that the tongue has the power of life and death. Telling an ex-boyfriend that you are bettering yourself solely to demonstrate a gross lack of judgment on the part of those who had considered you inferior is just not speaking life.

David was silent for several seconds before he answered.

"Shayna, that's not why I bought it for you."

We both knew he was lying.

As I ran my finger over the familiar handwriting in his letter, I was still smiling. I missed him. I missed the way his writing looked. Just having a letter in my hands brought me joy.

In his concluding comments, he asked for the software again, so I pulled out my newest stationery. It was blue and green cardstock with an inspirational quote by Maya Angelou at the top. I ruminated over what to say and let myself become enraptured in the thought of authoring a letter back.

I started mentally planning my comments and decided that in addition to the software CDs, I would also burn a music CD for David. With the bitterness and hurt from the breakup starting to dissolve, I wanted to express my gratitude for our relationship and apologize for how I might have failed him during the past year.

A week passed without my having time to write the letter. But I didn't want David to think I was ignoring him. I copped out on the old-world romanticism of a letter and dialed David's cell phone instead. He didn't answer, so I left a voicemail. I tried to be polite and cheerful in the recording, but I couldn't help wondering why David hadn't answered. I had dialed not one but *two* different numbers.

The following day, there was a voicemail on my home office line.

"Hi Shayna, it's David. I got your message last night. Sorry, I didn't recognize the number . . ." He paused in midsentence, as if realizing he had divulged too much. "I switched phones and didn't transfer my phone book."

I replayed the message a second time. I didn't believe him.

"Isn't that sort of a weird thing to say? Why would he say that?" I asked Sessa a few minutes later. "He deleted my numbers from his phone, didn't he," I said sadly. Sessa didn't respond, and I already knew the answer.

I wanted to collapse and start bawling. I couldn't conceive of being just some other girl in David's life. Just a set of numbers to be deleted from a phone book. He had told me when we first started dating that there was a "forty-eight-hour rule." The boy has forty-eight hours after receiving the girl's number to call. Once he leaves a message, if she doesn't respond within forty-eight hours, he deletes her phone number. Since it had taken me more than forty-eight hours to respond after David's initial phone call a year earlier, my number had to be reprogrammed before our first date.

"I don't want to sound paranoid," I continued. "But I think David already started seeing someone else."

"I think that's probably true," Sessa quickly responded.

The rapidity and confidence with which Sessa delivered her reply made me wonder if she didn't *think* that it was true so much as *know* that it was. After all, Sessa's brother is good friends with David. It was through the two of them that Sessa and I met.

I chose not to press Sessa for more information and instead, retreated to my room. I felt crippled and ill-equipped to handle the loneliness welling up. Tears started cascading down my cheeks.

I replayed the message over and over in my head. He had called me "Shayna" and not a silly nickname. From the moment we had started dating, I had rarely, if ever, heard my actual name. I was "Sweetie" or "Sweetheart" or "Quiggy" to David. My name was foreign on his lips. Even after we had broken up, voicemails or e-mails started with "Hey you" or "Hey there."

He never called me "Shayna."

I used to save the text messages and voicemails that David sent to me. Messages that would beep on my way to work in Hagerstown wishing me luck at a board meeting. Or beeps that awakened me out of half-sleep to say Good night as he left his office at one or two in the morning. I kept the voicemails that he left while driving, telling me that he loved me. I used to replay them and tarry over the way his voice sounded, how he said "I love you," the way he used to put "my" in front of pet names. "Good night, *my* Sweetheart." "Good luck, *my* Quiggy."

David's final instruction in the voicemail was to call him back, but I couldn't bring myself to do it. He told me that I could mail the software he wanted to either his office or his P.O. Box. There was no mention of mailing it to him at home. No thought of dropping it off. It was a bruising realization. I wouldn't know what to say if I called back.

Instead, I will thoughtfully compose a letter next week. I will mail it with the software to the address that David requested. I will take deep breaths, and I will wipe away my tears. I will believe that it's OK that I ended a relationship with a man who loved me, but whose family would never accept me. I will not despair because David has moved on faster than I could. I will trust that my decision to not date again until this summer is a positive one.

I deleted the voicemail on my home office line. Tomorrow, I'll consider what to do with the twenty text messages still on my cell phone.

Encounter the Word

"But I will sing of your strength, in the morning I will sing of your love; for you are my fortress, my refuge in times of trouble. O my Strength, I sing praise to you; you, O God, are my fortress, my loving God" (Psalm 59:16, 17, NIV).

Encounter

+ Where do you typically turn to for refuge in the midst of heartache and despair?
+ How can GOD offer you support? What meaningful things might He be saying to you in empathizing with your experience?
+ What role do you want GOD to fulfill in the midst of your troubles? Talk with Him and discover His intentions.

5.45 Storms

(Lynell LaMountain)

What storms are you going through?

If there was a particular storm in your life you could point to and say, "Peace, be still," which one would it be?

Psalm 93 is about storms. And it begins with these reassuring words: "The Lord reigns, he is robed in majesty; the Lord is robed in majesty and is armed with strength. The world is firmly established; it cannot be moved. Your throne was established long ago; you are from eternity" (verses 1, 2, NIV).

Sometimes we panic when we face storms. Large waves taller than buildings heave and roll toward us, filling our heart with fear. Living in fear is a horrible existence. It can be big fears like financial stuff, or relational fears, or fear of doing the right thing because of the consequences.

That's why I want you to know today that our GOD is stronger than any of your storms: "Mightier than the thunder of the great waters, mightier than the breakers of the sea—the Lord on high is mighty" (Psalm 93:4, NIV).

Nothing can destabilize GOD. Nothing.

Which means that nothing can destabilize you. Nothing.

GOD's rule and reign are stable; His rule and reign in your life are stable; His word is stable; and you are stable in the storm.

Jesus calmed the storm in Mark 4:39, when he said, " 'Quiet! Be still!' Then the wind died down and it was completely calm" (NIV).

You and I worship a GOD who can calm any storm to which we point.

He calms the storm.

Not us.

Him.

So cast all of the weight of your worry upon Him right now, and enjoy the peace He offers. He wants you to ask Him to calm your storms. He's waiting to make your life completely calm right now.

Encounter the Word

After reading all of Psalm 93, give special attention and meditation to the following passage:

"Mightier than the thunder of the great waters, mightier than the breakers of the sea—the Lord on high is mighty" (Psalm 93:4, NIV).

Encounter

+ What areas of your life could use some "stabilizing"? Talk these over with GOD.
+ How do you typically react to the storms of life? What role might GOD want to play in these turbulent times?
+ What challenges do you have in asking for help? From others? From GOD?
+ Do you believe you can handle the storms on your own? Elaborate.

5.5 Check Your Water Gun

(Lynell LaMountain)

A lot can be said for seizing the day and living fearlessly. But before we all shout "Yeah GOD!" and charge hell with our water pistols, I thought maybe we should remind ourselves of some action steps that biblical heroes took to guarantee victory (because there's nothing quite like the feeling of charging hell only to find that your water pistol is empty).

Biblical heroes did the following:

1. Always, always, always prayed first and asked GOD to reveal His perfect will for them and their situation.

They knew that He desired them to be successful, prosperous, and happy (it's in His covenant—Genesis 15).

2. They received and implemented GOD's plan.

Noah and the ark, Moses and the Red Sea, Joshua and Jericho, David and Goliath, Samson and Delilah (OK, bad example), but you get the idea . . . Point is, they didn't rely on a limited point of view that was based on "common sense." Seas don't part; cities don't crumble at the sound of trumpet blasts; and boys don't kill giants.

3. They sized-up the situation as they planned, and adjusted accordingly to changing circumstances.

4. They didn't impose their will upon GOD and say, "GOD wills it!"

Faith keeps us in step with GOD, whereas presumption expects GOD to keep step with us.

5. When the time was right, they launched their plan.

But let me say this: people usually wait too long to take action. Procrastination is a delaying tactic that many people use, and it usually goes something like this: "Let's pray about it . . ." Prayerless action is bad. But so is "prayerful" inaction.

Here's what I think: if people prayed as much as they said they did, then there would be a lot more action and forward progress in their lives, because GOD is able, capable, and on the move. He's ready to lead us into the Promised Land, but we're dragging our sandals in the wilderness wasteland.

It's interesting to me that many of the heroes of the Bible felt horribly unprepared (does the name Gideon ring a bell?). It was during life's circumstances, struggles, and trials that GOD had prepared them to rely upon Him—to trust His power even when it looked like they were going to die—especially when it looked like they were going to die.

They knew that GOD could only do for them what He could do through them—but only as they took action. So they jumped off the cliff when GOD said "Jump," and worked with Him in building their wings on the way down.

Encounter the Word

After reading Daniel 3, give special attention and meditation to the following passage:

"If we are thrown into the blazing furnace, the God we serve is able to save us from it, and he will rescue us from your hand, O king. But even if he does not, we want you to know, O king, that we will not serve your gods or worship the image of gold you have set up" (Daniel 3:17, 18, NIV).

Encounter

+ Do you find yourself consulting with GOD about your plans or consulting with GOD about His plans? Elaborate.
+ When have you taken a leap of faith? What did GOD reveal to you in the midst of that experience and its aftermath?
+ What action steps are you being prompted toward as a result of your conversations with Christ?

5.55 He Already Knows

(Lynell LaMountain)

Do you ever have trouble getting your point across? You communicate the best you can, but still the other person doesn't seem to get it?

I'm glad that's not the way it is with GOD, aren't you?

Even if we have trouble telling Him what's on our hearts, or communicating our wants and needs to Him, we can be sure that He understands.

"Don't worry and ask yourselves, 'Will we have anything to eat? Will we have anything to drink? Will we have any clothes to wear?' Only people who don't know God are always worrying about such things. Your Father in heaven knows that you need all of these" (Matthew 6:31, 32, CEV). Before you even ask, GOD knows what you want. Before you even ask, He understands your needs. And before you even ask, His blessings are on the way.

Your Part

If GOD already knows and understands our needs and wants before we even ask, as noted in Matthew 6:31, 32, then, besides asking, what else are we supposed to do?

I'm glad you asked, because experiencing GOD's blessings and a meaningful, satisfying reality goes beyond mere asking. We must do something else too. The secret is found in Psalm 23:1–3. First, I want to share the New International Version, and then *The Message* paraphrase:

"The LORD is my shepherd, I shall not be in want. He makes me lie down in green pastures, he leads me beside quiet waters, he restores my soul. He guides me in paths of righteousness for his name's sake" (NIV).

In those verses, do you see *all* the things GOD does *for us?*

What do you see as your job in the process of receiving?

Your job (mine too) is to allow GOD to *lead* you. If you allow Him to lead you, He'll give you the desires of your heart.

Here's *The Message* paraphrase of Psalm 23:1–3.

"God, my shepherd! I don't need a thing. You have bedded me down in lush meadows, you find me quiet pools to drink from. True to your word, you let me catch my breath and send me in the right direction."

Encounter the Word

After reading all of chapter 6 in Matthew, give special attention and meditation to the following passage:

"Therefore I tell you, do not worry about your life, what you will eat or drink; or about your body, what you will wear. Is not life more important than food, and the body more important than clothes? Look at the birds of the air; they do not sow or reap or store away in barns, and yet your heavenly Father feeds them. Are you not much more valuable than they? Who of you by worrying can add a single hour to his life?" (Matthew 6:25–27, NIV).

Encounter

+ When have you felt that GOD just doesn't understand your needs? Elaborate.
+ How are you allowing GOD to lead you? In what aspects of your life do you sometimes wrestle with GOD for control?
+ What gradual steps can to you take with GOD to gain freedom from worry? Talk over these steps with Him.

5.6 Why I Won't Get Into Graduate School: Reason #34 (Written Jan. 12)

(Shayna Bailey)

"Dear Applicant, we regret to inform you that you have failed to produce sufficient evidence of your academic proficiency, professional excellence, and soundness of charac-ter. As you did not submit the three required recommendation letters needed to process your application, your application was rendered incomplete and we have no choice but to

deny you admittance to our institution . . ."

I thought it was a fabulous idea to give my recommenders self-addressed priority mail envelopes before I headed to my mother's house in South Florida for Christmas. In fact, I knew it was. I drove to the main post office in downtown Baltimore early one morning in December, purchased postage for the envelopes, and didn't even feel guilty about calling in to work late. The holidays were approaching, and I knew that the priority postage was a good investment.

When I had only received one of the three sets of letters I needed by December 29, though, I started getting nervous. My own deadlines weren't until January 1, but most schools wanted them submitted with my application, *not* separately.

I called J. C., my friend and former boss. Then I left a message at an old professor's office. J. C. was the first to call back.

"I mailed them a few days ago," he told me. "I'm surprised you don't have them by now."

"OK, well don't worry about it," I replied. "As long as I get them by the second of January, it'll be fine. Even if I have to pick them up and mail them out again the same day, it's fine."

Except, it wasn't fine. January 2 came and went. Then, January 3. I was forced to mail incomplete applications, but I reasoned that both envelopes couldn't possibly arrive after January 4. When my former professor called back, he said that he had even *overnighted* them to expedite the process.

On January 4, I flew back to Baltimore without having received either set of letters. January 5, 6, and 7 passed.

"I finally talked to the post office today," my mother told me on Monday. "The postmaster forwarded J. C.'s letters to Maryland. Your other envelope is here in Florida, but they won't let me sign for it because it's in your name."

"Are you kidding me?" I shrieked.

"Don't worry, I'll figure out a way to get the envelope here. Just wait on J. C.'s to get to you in Maryland," she advised me.

So, I did wait. January 8 and 9 passed.

On Tuesday night, Sessa appeared in the doorway of my bedroom as I was sprawled out on my bed in front of my laptop. I had been visibly stressed about the situation all day.

"Still no sign of the recommendations?" she asked.

"Nope. My mother said they were forwarded back to Maryland, but the last time I had a forwarding address . . ."

Suddenly, I realized it. The last time I had a forwarding address from my mother's house in Florida, it was more than a year ago. In fact, I had had so many forwarding addresses while living in Baltimore that I couldn't even know where J. C.'s letters would have gone. All I knew was that they weren't coming to my current address.

The next morning, I started calling and e-mailing schools to explain my situation. I had been delaying the calls because I had no viable explanation. Were the recommendation letters here in Maryland? In Florida? In Michigan?

The postal service has never really done me justice with the forward. For the entire time that I was in college and my sister was in graduate school in Michigan, we would regularly receive each other's mail. Wrong name, wrong forward, wrong state. This was precisely the reason that I had cancelled any forwards in my name.

"Well, *if* we choose to hold your application," an admissions officer told me, "you will be assessed a late fee. Before we make that determination, though, you need to formally request an extension and give us a date when you are certain your application will be complete."

I quickly composed the e-mail, set the date for January 16, and hit "Send." I knew the professor's recommendations were on their way (because my mother is *not* the postal service!), and I assumed that J. C. could print a new set of recommendation letters more quickly than I could ascertain the location of the original set. A few minutes later, I called J. C. at work.

"I'm sorry," J. C.'s assistant informed me. "J. C. is out of town until the . . . twenty-second, I believe."

J. C. hadn't mentioned going out of town when we talked before New Year's. Even if he was gone, though, we were close enough as friends for me to request an interruption in his vacation. The only times he doesn't answer my calls are during family emergencies or when he is out of state.

I called his cell phone. It went to voicemail.

"I seriously can't believe this is happening!" I announced to Sessa. I was actually going to miss a deadline I set myself.

Sessa smiled. "Maybe you'll have to stay in Maryland," she said innocently. "You can always go back to Hopkins and keep living with me."

I rolled my eyes and headed to the hallway closet to grab my coat. J. C. might be in the midst of a family or other emergency, but he had written a set of letters already, and I was going to find them.

I drove to a row house I lived in during the fall of 2005 and rang the doorbell. There was no answer, so I went back the next day. January 10 passed.

I went to my branch post office and inquired about where mail would potentially get sent if it was forwarded to an incorrect address.

"Well, it would get returned to the sender," I was told.

"And what happens if there's no return address?"

"It goes to a dead mail center in Atlanta. You have to write to them to request the package."

"What if I don't have enough time for that to happen?"

"I'm sorry, but there is no other way to contact the dead mail center."

I was kicking myself for having only put my Florida address on the envelopes. I had no idea whether or not J. C. had put his return address on the package. Even if he had, he was also out of town for the holidays, and I didn't know what address he would have written. I called his office again and left a message.

Thankfully, the professor's letters finally arrived on January 11. If J. C. cannot be contacted by the weekend, though, a certain roommate might or might not offer to author a recommendation letter that might or might not require impersonation, misrepresentation, and forgery for its construction.[1]

"Dear Applicant, we regret to inform you that due to your egregious breach in the ethical standards to which we hold our applicants and current students, we have no choice but to render your application fraudulent and deny you admittance to our institution . . ."

Encounter the Word

"God, my shepherd! I don't need a thing. You have bedded me down in lush meadows, you find me quiet pools to drink from. True to your word, you let me

---

1. This is, of course, a joke.

catch my breath and send me in the right direction" (Psalm 23:1–3, *The Message*).

Encounter

+ When in your life has "everything" seemed to go wrong? What was your reaction?
+ What role does prayer play for you in these types of circumstances? How close to "desperate" do you need to be in order to resort to prayer? Elaborate.
+ Exhausted from the complexity of real life? How might you ask GOD for refreshment?

5.65 Here's Some Power

(Lynell LaMountain)

When was the last time you were so weary you felt like sitting down and closing your eyes for a year? Or your mind felt like a gob of marshmallow-slathered sweet potato casserole?

Truth is, there are times when we walk with GOD and then there are times when we need Him to carry us—mentally, physically, emotionally, or spiritually.

Today is one of those days for me.

Here's a promise with some power for us:

"But he [GOD] said to me [Paul], 'My grace is sufficient for you, for my power is made perfect in weakness.' Therefore I will boast all the more gladly about my weaknesses, so that Christ's power may rest on me" (2 Corinthians 12:9, NIV).

Paul had been dealing with what he called a "thorn in the flesh"—something that he says GOD had allowed into his life to keep him from becoming spiritually arrogant.

He asked GOD to remove the "thorn." (We're not sure what it was. Some say it was bad eyesight from when he was blinded by GOD's glory on the road to Damascus.) But GOD didn't remove it. Why? Because it was to remind Paul of his constant need of GOD's power.

So, if weariness is your thorn today, then this is a great opportunity to realize that we're not invincible and that our success isn't solely tied to our energy stores. GOD is our Success, Supply, Surplus and, most important for me today, our Strength.

Claim this promise as a present reality and see the difference it makes in your life now:

"God is our refuge and strength, an ever-present help in trouble" (Psalm 46:1, NIV).

Right now, say to yourself, "Thank You, GOD, for being my Refuge and Strength, and for giving me Your power and help to win the day."

Encounter the Word

After reading all of chapter 46 in Psalms, give special attention and meditation to the following passage:

"I love you, O LORD, my strength. The LORD is my rock, my fortress and my deliverer; my God is my rock, in whom I take refuge. He is my shield and the horn of my salvation, my stronghold" (Psalm 18:1, 2, NIV).

Encounter

+ Have you had an injury or illness where you have had to rely on others for help? What was difficult about that experience for you?
+ What are the "thorns" in your life? How might these keep you from becoming arrogant?
+ Where in your life might you need GOD's refuge? Let Him know your desire.

5.7 On Not Abandoning Hope Prematurely (Written Two Days Later, Sunday, Jan. 14)

(Shayna Bailey)

Voicemail received today:

"Hi Shayna, it's your sister. I think I found something that you might have been looking for . . . your recommendation letters? They just got here [in Michigan]. Your story just gets stranger and stranger, doesn't it?"

And this, my friend, is why I don't even try to be a fiction writer. I couldn't fabricate stories like this if I tried! We have surmised that the letters were mailed from Maryland to Florida, then forwarded to my sister's new address in western Michigan—where she has, incidentally, never had a forward set up. We also don't know where the letters have been for the past two weeks. Anyway, as Providence would have it, we have a single day to overnight the letters, and we will, in fact, make the January 16 deadline. Again, I couldn't make it up if I tried.

Encounter the Word

"For I know the plans I have for you, declares the Lord, plans to prosper you and not to harm you, plans to give you a hope and future" (Jeremiah 29:11, NIV).

Encounter

+ What do you believe are GOD's intentions for you?
+ What is your initial reaction when things don't go as you planned?
+ How will you know His intentions? You might bring it up in your discussions with Him.

5.75 How Do You React?

(Lynell LaMountain)

How well do you cope with unfavorable circumstances? I'm talking about significant circumstances that have the potential to change your life direction, circumstances that alter your relationships, your career, your finances . . . how well do you cope with the unexpected?

Life happens.

Events transpire that drop your stomach into a briny pool of fear. Your heart overheats with anxiety. And your mind becomes a tempest of liquid worry as you picture the worst. Be honest with me: when this happens, you're tempted to force your desired outcome, aren't you?

People say it all the time, "Make it happen!" (I really hate that arrogant, manipulative mantra.)

It's one thing to "make" something happen, to force a situation through sheer human will and clever effort. But it's another thing to prepare the way for GOD to make something happen through you (by the way, as a rule of thumb, you will have to invest action in this process).

One of my favorite promises for this kind of situation is Exodus 14:13, 14, because it strengthens my faith and empowers my resolve, and it'll do the same for you.

Moses had just led the Israelites out of Egypt.

The Red Sea was ahead of them.

The Egyptian army was behind them.

The mountains and desert flanked 'em.

But this is what GOD had Moses tell His people:

"Do not be afraid. Stand firm and you will see the deliverance the Lord will bring you today. The Egyptians you see today you will never see again. The Lord will fight for you; you need only to be still" (NIV).

When it appears that your circumstances are working against you, remember that GOD is *always* working *for* you. React to His unfailing power and not to your circumstances.

There's nothing in your life that stumps Him. Nothing in your life that worries Him. Nothing in your life that overpowers Him. Get it? Good.

Trust GOD and move forward. If you don't know what that means for your life, then ask Him. And He'll show you.

When you respond and move forward, even if it's just one small step, miracles will begin happening. The sea will part. Or the mountains will move. And your deliverance will be sealed.

Encounter the Word

After reading Psalm 27, give special attention and meditation to the following passage:

"The LORD is my light and my salvation—whom shall I fear? The LORD is the stronghold of my life—of whom shall I be afraid?" (Psalm 27:1, NIV).

Encounter

+ When surrounded by what seems to be insurmountable obstacles, what is your reaction?
+ What fears are reinforced when the odds seem stacked against you?
+ Where in your life do you want to start having GOD step you through? Discuss it with Him.

5.8 Believing[2]

(Shayna Bailey)

A couple of years ago, the city of Baltimore started a campaign called "Believe."

---

2. Entry was blogged September 30, 2005.

The city printed bumper stickers, banners, and posters with an all-black background and plain white letters that said "Believe" in the middle.

The aim of the campaign was to raise awareness about drug use and decrease drug trafficking, usage, and related violence. With such a powerful message, though, the bumper stickers gained popularity quickly. You can see the "Believe" memorabilia almost anywhere you look, and a restaurant in my area of town even starting printing their own bumper sticker, reading "Believe, Hon."

A lot of people ask me why I believe in GOD. Depending on who the person is and how well I know them, I might recount specific faith experiences that demonstrated the undeniable presence of GOD in my life. I might talk about what it feels like to have quiet devotion moments or the profound realizations that I have about GOD's love for me. There are usually so many reasons, however, that it's hard to choose only a few and to be concise in my explanations.

Believing can only happen with faith, though. Hebrews 11:1 says that faith is "being sure of what we hope for and certain of what we do not see" (NIV). Furthermore, Philippians 4:7 describes the peace of GOD as "transcend[ing] all understanding." In short, it's being able to "just know" (NIV).

We all have a need to believe in something, which is probably a central reason for the popularity of the "Believe" campaign. Where does your faith come from? Why do you believe in GOD?

Encounter the Word

"I am not ashamed of the gospel, because it is the power of God for the salvation of everyone who believes: first for the Jew, then for the Gentile. For in the gospel a righteousness from God is revealed, a righteousness that is by faith from first to last, just as it is written: 'The righteous will live by faith' " (Romans 1:16–18, NIV).

Encounter

+ What role does prayer have in the developing and maturing of your faith?
+ How have your conversations with Christ fostered a spiritual intuition or "just knowing" perception in your life?
+ What message does your belief in GOD convey to your friends and family? Your colleagues? Your enemies?

5.9 This Is Difficult

(Lynell LaMountain)

What tempts you to stop trusting and relying on GOD?

What kinds of things need to happen before you usually start having second thoughts about His leadership in your life?

For the children of Israel who wandered in the desert for forty years, it was usually thirst, hunger, or a lack of security that made their faith crack.

In fact, when you read Exodus, you'll find them yearning for Egypt. They had more faith in Pharaoh as their provider than they had in GOD! Their lives were miserable and their children were slaves but, hey, at least there were steaks in the freezer. They toiled away making another nation rich while wasting away in the fields, enduring beatings, all so they could have a bowl of Cheerios waiting for them at breakfast.

Ever wonder why GOD led the Israelites through the desert through a land of lack and bareness? It was to teach them that all they needed was Him. As long as they relied on Him and responded to His guidance in their lives by taking essential action, they prospered and were happy.

Each of us has our own wilderness experience, when we're tempted to trust some other source as our provider; and many times that other source is ourselves. It's a hard thing to describe, but trusting GOD isn't always easy. When you can't see beyond the diagnosis, or the mountain of bills, or the loss of a loved one—when loss and uncertainty crash down upon you—it's not easy to let go, especially when your instinct to struggle through is so strong.

When Jesus was on the verge of death in the wilderness and Satan tempted Him by suggesting He turn the stones into bread, Jesus said, "Man shall not live by bread alone but by every word that proceeds from the mouth of GOD."

What that means is: first comes trust, then comes dinner. Why settle for bread and water when GOD has a feast for you, a feast that's on the other side of uncertainty.

I'm not sure what you're going through right now, but would you consider joining me in asking GOD this question: "Father, what do You want me to learn today?" I've found that this question tends to focus me more on GOD and less on myself.

Ultimately, whatever we're going through boils down to this (and trust me, this is where GOD leads the vast majority of us as He fortifies our character): will we trust Him as our Provider, Sustainer, and Deliverer, even when the situation is grim (and even when it's not grim)? Will we follow Him into the darkness?

When your situation is the darkest, you're only a few steps away from your miracle. So, keep walking. Trust GOD through the night. Follow the path He illuminates for you. And one day soon, you'll step into your Promised Land of rest, abundance, and eternal joy.

Encounter the Word

After reading all of chapter 17 in 1 Kings, give special attention and meditation to the following passage:

" 'As surely as the Lord your God lives,' she replied, 'I don't have any bread—only a handful of flour in a jar and a little oil in a jug. I am gathering a few sticks to take home and make a meal for myself and my son, that we may eat it—and die.' . . .

"The Lord heard Elijah's cry, and the boy's life returned to him, and he lived. Elijah picked up the child and carried him down from the room into the house. He gave him to his mother and said, 'Look, your son is alive!'

"Then the woman said to Elijah, 'Now I know that you are a man of God and that the word of the Lord from your mouth is the truth' " (1 Kings 12:22–24, NIV).

Encounter

+ What are the dire circumstances that you have experienced? Where or when have you found yourself low on the basic necessities for life and your faith stretched?
+ What is your cry to GOD?

5.95 Frustrated

(Lynell LaMountain)

Have you ever been frustrated by not knowing what to do next in a given situation? I think everyone has. Can you imagine always knowing what to do and being able to identify the essential course of action?

I've been wrestling with GOD in the area of wisdom. I want more of it. I want His wisdom. I want to see things as He sees them. I want His understanding. I want to know what to do next that will manifest my desires and His will in my life.

Probably that's why I've been thinking about King Solomon in the back of my mind this week. He craved wisdom more than air. And I think that's where we have to be. We have to *crave* it. Be obsessed about it.

I'm talking about practical knowledge that magnifies and advances GOD's power internally and externally. Solomon wrote these words in Proverbs 2:6: "For the Lord gives wisdom, and from his mouth come knowledge and understanding" (NIV). Solomon identifies the source for us. But He also reveals the value we must place on obtaining it:

"My son, if you accept my words and store up my commands within you, turning your ear to wisdom and applying your heart to understanding, and if you call out for insight and cry aloud for understanding, and if you look for it as for silver and search for it as for hidden treasure, then you will understand the fear of the Lord and find the knowledge of God" (Proverbs 2:1–5, NIV).

In my book, that's a promise. And I claim it in the name of Jesus.

Are you craving wisdom in any particular area of your life? Then GOD is your goldmine of understanding. Go to Him and start digging. Understanding is something that's earned. There's effort involved. Just as you wrestled to understand chemistry or physics or geometry—you earned it.

I think we should commit ourselves to the effort it will take to understand the knowledge of GOD, don't you? Can you imagine understanding the power that spoke our world into existence? That glued galaxies to the heavens? The power that breathed life into man?

That's exactly what's being offered to us. And in understanding this power, I have a hunch that understanding our lives and what to do next ought to be pretty easy. "The fear of the Lord is the beginning of knowledge, but fools despise wisdom and discipline" (Proverbs 1:7, NIV).

Claim This One

After reading Psalm 67 this morning in my spiritual focusing time, I was shuffling through my 3x5 cards (on which I've written promises to claim), and I found this one (which I claimed for myself), and which I now feel impressed to share with you: "Show me your ways, O Lord, teach me your paths. Guide me in your truth and teach me, for you are God my Savior, and my hope is in you all day long" (Psalm 25:4, 5, NIV).

This verse teaches several principles, but here are a couple of them: (1) GOD *is* the answer you're looking for in your situation; and (2) GOD *has* the answer you're looking for and He's *willing* to share it.

What problems do you have? What challenges do you face? What major decisions do you need to make? In what areas of your life do you need clarity?

I encourage you to claim this promise (which really is an invitation), and GOD *will* speak to you. Open the pages of the Bible today and see where the Holy Spirit leads your study. Also, don't underestimate the power of your gut. I really believe that the Holy Spirit speaks to us through our intuition, through that sixth sense. What does your "gut" say you should do?

One more thing before I go. I've found it helpful to meditate on the situation while I'm sleepy and have gone to bed for the night, and to specifically ask for GOD's guidance or solution. You'll be amazed at how often you wake up knowing exactly what you need to do.

Encounter the Word

After reading all of chapter 6 in Matthew, give special attention and meditation to the following passages:

"But if from there you seek the LORD your God, you will find him if you look for him with all your heart and with all your soul" (Deuteronomy 4:29, NIV).

"Be joyful always; pray continually; give thanks in all circumstances, for this is God's will for you in Christ Jesus" (1 Thessalonians 5:16–18, NIV).

Encounter

+ What is your source of wisdom, confidence, and direction?
+ With whom do you confer to give you a sense of purpose and meaning?
+ What role has GOD played in your life? Has the depth and quantity of conversation with GOD reflected the role you want Him to have with you?

+ What steps will you take today to seek GOD out and experience His will for your life?

My Experience

_____
_____
_____
_____
_____
_____
_____
_____
_____
_____
_____
_____
_____
_____
_____
_____
_____
_____
_____

6.0 **SABBATH**

6.1 Embrace Sabbath as Soul CPR

It is our desire to experience GOD's Sabbath rest on the seventh day and beyond. We're learning to make the invisible Spirit tangible in the visible realm. Rest, GOD's restoration and renewal, forms the rhythm of life. We desire GOD to "re-create" His Spirit in us.

6.2 Sacred Space: Learning the Rhythms of Grace

(A. Allan Martin)

My daughter likes to camp out. We take broomsticks (or any long sticks we can find in the garage), those office "pincher" clips, string, and the largest bed-sheet we can "borrow" from the linen closet. With some masterful daddy-daughter engineering we create a tent in her bedroom. Under the canopy of this king-size shelter, we bring all the camping necessities: flashlights, all our favorite pillows and blankets, and the stuffed friends we wish to invite. The evening may start with flashlight races or finger shadow shows, but it always winds down with stories fresh from our imaginations, and slumber, sweet slumber.

"Daddy, pull out the trundle."

Her childhood twin bed isn't quite ready to accommodate Alexa, her mom, and me, but she is eager to have me close by, under the tent. So we pull out the trundle, and I rest with my girls. I love to listen to the giggles, the breaths, and then, the sleep.

It's almost magical to me—how an ordinary flat sheet anchored to the ceiling fan, taped to a mop stick and draped over my daughter's bed, can create such a different space from the space "out there," where chores, homework, and cell phones hold dominion. It's a wonderful, mysterious place—a sacred space.

It reminded me of a quote from author and speaker Terry Hershey: "We live in a world of two spaces. In one space is born productivity, activity and busyness. In the other, a sanctuary for renewal, reflection and Sabbath."[1]

If only I could take that magical bedsheet and somehow drape it over my dizzy-paced life! There are too many things to do, and time is so limited. Rushing through the hours, I find myself often lacking the efficiency to squeeze any more productivity out of the minutes. I am driven to succeed, and the necessary pace has little space for storytelling or silly finger rabbits etched by flashlights on the fabric sky.

Most of my life is spent in one space, where there is much work and little time. I find that deceptive promise in the back of my head, seducing me to work harder and longer, so that when I get it all done, then I can "kick back and take it easy." So I go faster and faster, like a stereotypical husband, who, in his heart, knows he's lost but refuses to stop and ask for directions. As if going faster will somehow help me resolve the lostness; faster, faster, faster I go.

The speed of life refuses to slow, even though I know that important life stuff is starting to blur. I find it difficult to let off the gas. Overnight packages, instant messaging, and global walkie-talkies have left their mark. I live life feeling tardy for it, always catching up to where I think I ought to be. "Gotta run" has become more of a lifestyle than a catch phrase.

In my heart I resonate with John Jerome's words: "I was running past the high: Hurrying past the very transcendent moments I was seeking."[2] Is there any relief from the tiring pace, this insane treadmill of demands and deadlines? Before I lose anymore important moments . . . where can I stop and ask for directions?

---

1. Quoted in *A Few Things That Matter* electronic newsletter, vol. 11, June 24, 2005, http://www.terryhershey.com/nl-sanctuary-1.htm.

2. Quoted in *A Few Things That Matter* electronic newsletter, vol. 7, February 28, 2005, http://www.terryhershey.com/nl-stillness-2.htm.

That's when Eugene Peterson's paraphrase of a Scripture passage offered me a GPS to sacred space: "Are you tired? Worn out? Burned out on religion? Come to me. Get away with me and you'll recover your life. I'll show you how to take a real rest. Walk with me and work with me—watch how I do it. Learn the unforced rhythms of grace. I won't lay anything heavy or ill-fitting on you. Keep company with me and you'll learn to live freely and lightly" (Matthew 11:28–30, *The Message*).

Get Away With Me

Am I tired? Yes. Worn out? Yes. Burned out on religion? Yes. The words of the passage sound like an invitation from Jesus to join Him in a different place. A different pace. A sacred space.

Musical artist Jimmy Buffet captures well the change of pace:

"Most of the time fish are swimming around either eating or avoiding being eaten."

"I know a lot of humans that do the same thing."

"But fish know they need a break from the cycle of the food chain, and it happens at slack tide."

"So it's kind of a universal time-out?"

"I call it Quiet Time, people would be better off if they did the same."[3]

Jesus beckons me to a quiet time, a hammock for my heart where I can "recover my life." Weary of swimming in circles, I am drawn to His offer to experience real rest. But every fiber in my responsible, industrious, over-achieving being resists the notion of quiet time.

"Quiet time?"

"There's no such thing," says my calendar. "However, the reality of your 9:00, 10:00, and 11:30 are right here."

My laptop pipes in, "Have you seen how many e-mails demand your immediate attention?"

---

3. Jimmy Buffet, *A Salty Piece of Land* (New York: Little, Brown, 2004), 292.

"Rest?" scoffs my cell phone. "That's what happens when you collapse on your bed after I'm done with you."

Theologian and pastor Eugene Peterson interrupts my conversation with my gadgets: "Many people simply cannot believe that there can be a large, leisurely center to life where GOD can be pondered. They doubt they can enter realms of spirit where wonder and adoration have a place to develop, and where play and delight have time to flourish. Is all this possible in our fast-paced lives? . . . The name for it is Sabbath."[4]

Slack tide is defined as a time of relatively still water at the turn of the tides. The sacred space of Sabbath offers me a slack tide, a space of quiet and stillness, where I can jump into the hammock with Jesus and simply adore spending time with Him. The constant, frenetic motion of my life is put on pause as I enjoy a time-out to develop delight and wonder.

Don't get me wrong, this isn't suggesting that Jesus is absent from the rest of my life. It's just that at slack tide, I am afforded the leisure of resting in Him, pondering the curious and creative aspects of His character. In this sacred space, I can enjoy His love for me, and He can receive my worship as a heartfelt gift. There is a centering that happens in this center of life, a recovery of what's most important, what is priceless. A different place. A different pace. A sacred space.

Unforced Rhythms of Grace

I've come to admit it. When it comes to the gift of rhythm, I was standing in the wrong line. My daughter, a ballerina and a pianist, has the gift. My wife can transform Kidz Praise into a holy dance party. To appease my wife, I have made a loose promise to "someday" take waltz lessons with her, but I don't see it happening. I'm lucky to remember my right from my left, and my goal has been to keep the two separate to prevent them from hurting each other.

That's how my life feels sometimes—an awkward stumble between action and reaction. Not in step with real life's heartbeat, it's easy to step on toes. Injury is inevitable. Mechanical and rushed, there's lots of dissonance and very little dance.

You might ask who's leading in this stuttering tango. That's a good question.

4. Quoted in *A Few Things That Matter* electronic newsletter, vol. 11, June 24, 2005, http://www.terryhershey.com/nl-sanctuary-1.htm.

Jesus says, "Walk with me and work with me—watch how I do it. Learn the unforced rhythms of grace."

I am one of those guys who doesn't like to read the instructions when I get a new gadget. You're lucky if I even glimpse at the "quick start steps" card. I've got the "I can figure it out" gene, and with some trial and error (and quadruple the time it would take to read and follow instructions), I can get almost any gadget running.

So, when Jesus asks me to walk and work and watch with Him, it's a little frustrating. I've been doing the religion thing for some time now. I've got the mechanics down pat and memorized enough Scriptures to win some awards. Why does He want me to walk with Him? What's the value of working with Him and watching how He does it? The dance of life seems pretty self-evident, so where's the value in learning from Him?

First, Jesus knows all the moves. He doesn't come at the dance of life without having experienced it to the very fullest. He knows where the peaks and valleys are; where the pace quickens, and where it comes to a dramatic halt. Jesus is not only able to lead me through the intricacies of the current steps; He is anticipating what's next. He knows the dance start to finish.

Second, Jesus is grace filled. Although Jesus could simply walk me through the dance of life and work with me, He's not satisfied with just teaching me the mechanics. Jesus wants me to experience graceful living. By watching Him, I see how even in the complicated sections of life's routine, Jesus exhibited grace, unexpected and lovely. He helps me learn His rhythm.

Third, Jesus wants to take the lead. It's not up to me to figure out the moves, to force the tempo, to complete the routine. I'm far more graceful and in step with real life when I allow Jesus to lead the dance. His timing is impeccable. His steps are decisive yet elegant. His rhythm brings healing beauty and gracefulness to my life.

I am caught off-guard by the grace exhibited. Instead of injury, I experience healing in this sacred space.

Wayne Muller, author of *Sabbath*, suggests, "Sabbath implies a willingness to be surprised by unexpected grace, to partake of those potent moments when creation renews itself, when what is finished inevitably recedes, and the sacred forces of healing astonish us with the unending promise of love and life."[5]

5. Wayne Muller, *Sabbath* (New York: Bantam, 1999).

A different place. A different pace. A sacred space.

Living Freely and Lightly

As I cultivate the sacred space of Sabbath in my life, I find it very different from the dread of yesteryear. To be honest, there had been times before in my life where Sabbath was a nuisance at best, drudgery at worst. My religious compulsion was to timekeep—scrambling to get all my stuff done before sunset. Then relying on my precise sunset calendar to let me know when I was to be released from the penitentiary of peaceful stillness. Time-out felt like a punishment. I had places to go. It felt like Sabbath was designed to entrap me, to demand my attention for a split second.

In my former opinion, Sabbath was devised to dictate motionlessness for proving a point. I couldn't compete in tennis tournaments; I didn't get to go to pep rallies or football games. Like a cousin's hand-me-down polyester leisure suit, which doesn't take into account Florida's humidity and the reality that one-size-*does-not*-fit-all, I had put up with Sabbath. It didn't fit me. I had people to see.

As I got older, I felt guilty for wanting to get it over with. I felt lazy if I took nap. I felt bridled by the inconvenience of observing this antiquated religious ritual. After all, this Sabbath thing was stunting my productivity. I had things to do.

New York Times columnist Verlyn Klinkenborg shares, "This is not how it's supposed to be, I know. I keep an endless mental list of the things that need to be done. But when a gray day comes, when the horses stand over their hay as though there were all the time in the world to eat it, one of the things that needs to be done is to sit still."[6] Could it be that, this "gray day," this sacred space was made for me? Could it be that in the stillness, GOD was tailoring a garment of grace that would allow my soul to breathe? Could it be that GOD was designing His wardrobe for human beings, not human "doings"?

Jesus says, "I won't lay anything heavy or ill-fitting on you. Keep company with me, and you'll learn to live freely and lightly." Contrary to my previous perceptions and practices, the sacred space of Sabbath offers freedom. I need the "gray day" to recapture all the time in the world. To savor a meal. To love deeply.

---

6. "At The Edge of the Visible," The Rural Life (column), *New York Times*, Nov. 6, 2004.

To be still and know GOD. There is liberation in the permission to live life in Jesus' presence, enjoying the custom fit of His acceptance and salvation, the play clothes of paradise.

A different place. A different pace. A sacred space.

Come to Me for Sacred Space

I hope my daughter never outgrows her love of "camping out." I love being able to design a shelter for her, even in her own room, where she feels safe and connected with us, where she enjoys our company, our stories, and wants her parents close.

I love those big hammocks! Have you seen them too? I am looking forward to lazy afternoons with my girls and some unrepentant napping. I hope to fulfill my wife's request and take waltz lessons with her. The effortless elegance of gracefully dancing in rhythm with the music will take time. I want to walk and work and watch, so I can learn.

I love the part of *The Sound of Music* when the von Trapp children don their custom-made play clothes produced by Maria. There is nothing better than comfortable clothes that give you the freedom to play.

It is with these ideas I am coming to Jesus so we can create our special sacred space. Like my daughter, I yearn for a little getaway, a place in my world where my Creator is especially close. I desire a hammock for my heart, a place where stories can be told and imagination is fostered; a space where I can recover my life and find real rest.

Like my girls, I'm eager to dance. I wish for a place and pace to really learn from Jesus, to watch His grace-fullness. I want to be in a space where He is leading and I experience the rhythm of His heart.

Like the von Trapp family, I'm into Designer play clothes. I'm in favor of a perfect fit, a place where I live freely and lightly. I want to be in His company, at a pace that allows me to enjoy the moments.

Jesus says, "Are you tired? Worn out? Burned out on religion? Come to me. Get away with me and you'll recover your life. I'll show you how to take a real rest. Walk with me and work with me—watch how I do it. Learn the unforced rhythms of grace. I won't lay anything heavy or ill-fitting on you. Keep company

with me and you'll learn to live freely and lightly."

He has it all figured out, custom designed, and ready for me. A different place. A different pace. A sacred space. He's inviting you too. Don't forget to bring your flashlight.

Encounter the Word

"Are you tired? Worn out? Burned out on religion? Come to me. Get away with me and you'll recover your life. I'll show you how to take a real rest. Walk with me and work with me—watch how I do it. Learn the unforced rhythms of grace. I won't lay anything heavy or ill-fitting on you. Keep company with me and you'll learn to live freely and lightly" (Matthew 11:28–30, *The Message*).

Encounter

- Where are the sacred spaces in your life? Where do you experience Sabbath?
- Where in your life do you need a bit of recovery? How have you involved Jesus in getting back your rhythm?
- What would it be like for you to live "freely and lightly"? Describe this type of life to a close friend. What is one small step you can take right now toward that way of life? Take it.

6.3 The Art of Being Still: A Work in Progress

(Lyris Bacchus-Steuber)

This past weekend I enjoyed an outdoor worship time with friends at Wekiva Springs State Park in Florida. A group of us hiked down to the springs after lunch; and on our way there, I saw a Muslim woman picnicking under a tree with her family. As our group passed by, she unrolled her prayer rug and, in front of everyone, knelt and said her prayers to Allah, facing east toward Mecca. I marveled at her devotion and reflected on how she does this five times per day.

I wish I had such devotion. Although I know that GOD is with me at all times, sometimes the busyness of everyday life gets in the way of my taking intentional time to acknowledge His presence. Decisions have to be made, clients need be seen, and paperwork completed. More often than I wish to acknowledge, I find myself falling into bed at 11:30 P.M. with a mumbled prayer, wishing I had spent more time communing with GOD. Luckily, I am thankful for GOD's grace and for the Holy Spirit, who makes my heart ache longingly for time with Him. And when I do take the time, I find myself always refreshed, longing for more.

Spending intentional time with GOD is a work in progress for me. I listen to Christian radio and talk with Him as I run to and from appointments. But the biggest challenge for me is to "be still." Psalm 46:10 (NIV), "Be still and know that I am GOD," is my benchmark.

Sometimes this is so hard to do when you have a list of things running through your mind of what you need to accomplish that day.

Here are some helpful hints for "being still."

First, identify a "sacred space" where you spend nonnegotiable time with GOD, free of distractions. Yes, that means turning off the cell phone! For some, this may be a special room in the house, the patio, under a tree in the yard, the car during your lunch break, or taking a walk.

Second, take some deep breaths, imagining Christ breathing the breath of life into you and you exhaling your cares.

Third, ask GOD to speak to you. If you choose to read Scripture, ask yourself what GOD might be telling you in that passage.

Next, learn to listen. If you find your mind wandering, slowly repeat the names of Jesus over and over again. When I have done this, I have never come away empty-handed. GOD may place a thought in your mind, remind you to pray for someone, or just let you be washed over with His joy and peace.

Encounter the Word

"Be still, and know that I am God; I will be exalted among the nations, I will be exalted in the earth. The Lord Almighty is with us; the God of Jacob is our fortress" (Psalm 46:10, 11, NIV).

Encounter

- ✦ What can you do to "be still" in the midst of your busy day?
- ✦ Where might you create your "sacred space"?
- ✦ What would a cell phone call from Jesus Christ be like for you? Explain.

6.4 How to Bruise a Bone . . . And Your Ego

(Shayna Bailey)

It was supposed to be a Sabbath afternoon like any other. We had sat through the morning church service, gorged ourselves on a feast at Aunt Vida's house, and even suffered through a second afternoon ceremony. Finally freed from the confines of a church sanctuary, my sister and J were eager to show us one of Michigan's claims to fame—the sand dunes.

I had actually visited the dunes when I was about six, when my Uncle Hurford was getting married. It had been simple to quickly climb the gargantuan mound of sand and run down again, screaming with delight. What my sister and J failed to tell us, however, was that they were not taking us to any six-year-old's sand dune. They were taking us to "the dune of death."

Just the approach to the dune was arduous. David and I lagged behind the group as we trudged through the sand on the shore of Lake Michigan. Gasping for air the entire time, we found ourselves having to take multiple breaks and nurse our exhaustion with the pitiful bottle of water we had in our possession.

When we finally arrived at the base of the dune, I was incredulous. "I don't remember the dunes being so steep," I whispered to David.

The scale of this dune was enormous. Just the height was intimidating, but it didn't nearly rival the grade of this thing. I could tell just by looking that climbing this dune was going to be like ascending a small mountain.

Deciding that my flip-flops would only be a detriment, I left them at the base of the dune and started climbing. My bare feet were slipping and sliding in the loose sand beneath me, but I dared not turn back to check my progress. If I saw the angle at which I was climbing, I would probably panic.

Finally at the top, we sat exhausted in the sand for several minutes, regaining our energy. The view was beautiful, and I wasn't ready to head back down again. My sister and J were the first back on their feet.

"I'm running down!" J yelled as my sister quickly followed behind him.

"Me too!"

As their figures grew smaller and farther away, we heard gleeful screams descending the dune. The other couple at the peak, Dan and Ayo, turned to us.

"I'm not running down," Ayo matter-of-factly declared. "These things scare me. Every time it's like a trust exercise of how reliable my husband is in getting me down safely."

I kind of wanted to run down like J and my sister, but the steepness was intimidating me. Finally committing to a decision, I turned to David.

"Why don't we just walk this time?"

J was already on his way back up for a second run, and we figured that we would be too, so David agreed. About halfway down the dune, however, David made a split-second decision.

"I'm going to start running," he told me, dropping my hand.

As he transformed into a flash of screaming brown, Ayo, Dan, and I watched David quickly disappear in front of us.

"I can't stop!" he was yelling.

Then, with a tumble and explosion of sand, David became a ball rolling down the side of the dune. The three of us erupted in laughter. If nothing else, this was going to be great bribery material for me. The mere sight of David tumbling to the foot of the dune was enough to keep me entertained for a while.

Then I noticed that David was not getting up.

J had turned back and was descending the dune to where David and my sister were. I couldn't see David, and it was clear that he hadn't stood up after his fall. I started walking faster, leaving Ayo and Dan behind me. When I reached David, he was covered in sand and clutching his left arm.

"I can't move it at all," he said with a wince. "I think it might be broken."

Four hours and several x-rays later, we determined that David's bone wasn't broken, but it was bruised.

For the next several days, I listened to David groan and complain about his arm. Even after we returned to Maryland, David was constantly whining in between doses of Vicodin.

"The doctor said it wasn't broken," I said indifferently, slightly annoyed at my boyfriend's childishness. I knew he was overreacting.

Two weeks later, however, I felt guilt washing over me as a new diagnosis was proclaimed.

The arm actually was broken, and David's pain was not in vain.

Encounter the Word

After reading Luke 8:22–25, give special attention and meditation to the following passage:

"The disciples went and woke him, saying, 'Master, Master, we're going to drown!' He got up and rebuked the wind and the raging waters; the storm subsided, and all was calm" (Luke 8:24, NIV).

Encounter

- Have you had times when life has simply run away with you? Elaborate.
- When the momentum of your work, studies, and obligations has refused to stop, what consequences has it had on you? What do you do when you feel like you are drowning?

6.45 Fasting From Faster

(A. Allan Martin)

Got a second?

It's incredible to me the pressure I have been put under to produce at light speed; it's almost like the microwave has always existed and I have never known a meal that wasn't nuked in less than 60 seconds. Sometimes I find myself way beyond the speed limit for no apparent reason, rushing to the next thing just because that has been the nature of my entire day. Multitasking is to be applauded, but something isn't quite right when I find myself and the drivers on either side of me talking on the cell phone and switching satellite radio stations all at the same time. Where is the sense in needing to be reachable at all times? I am amused by my colleagues who have a cell phone, a GPS, an iPod, and a PDA all strapped to their waist . . . I am sure it will create a great market for the superhero utility belt. I'm amused until I am jolted by my own vibrating, sing-songing Razr—deadlines have turned into dreadlines as the world seems to expect me to live a FedEx life; pressure to be able to have a quicker turn-around, more efficient time management, instantaneous results: at home, at work, at play, at weight loss, at relationships, at shopping, at education, at parenting, at lawn care, at ministry, at headache relief—it's almost as if the world is spinning faster on its axis . . . All I know is that this dizzying pace has got me nauseated . . . (deep breath).

Got a life?

So I will, today, fast from "faster."

"Be still."

I sit here listening, knowing that if His voice comes, it comes at its own savory pace.

There is anticipation, but I am refreshed knowing that it is based on GOD's timetable.

Stillness is calming.

"Be still, and know that I am God."

Slowly, I see Him as the best thing in my life.

The blur becomes focus.

With focus comes clarity.

He wants me.

He wants me to know Him.

To know Him is to love Him.

And I do.

"Be still, and know that I am God; I will be exalted among the nations, I will be exalted in the earth" (Psalm 46:10, NIV).

Got a Savior!

"Let my day bring You exaltation, LORD. Let my moments be stilled by Your Presence. Save me from speed. Slow my heart to beat with Yours. Let me experience awe. May You be exalted in my world. This is my worship to You today."

Encounter the Word

"My soul finds rest in God alone; my salvation comes from him" (Psalm 62:1, NIV).

"Create in me a pure heart, O God, and renew a steadfast spirit within me" (Psalm 59:10, NIV).

Encounter

- ✦ How fast are you going? What's driving you?
- ✦ Tell me about your vacations. Do you find yourself needing a vacation after your vacation? Elaborate.
- ✦ When do you take breaks or "fast" from the pace of life? How do you renew your spirit?

6.5 Come Away With Me

(A. Allan Martin)

"Are you tired? Worn out? Burned out on religion? Come to me. Get away with me and you'll recover your life. I'll show you how to take a real rest" (Matthew 11:28, The Message).

There's been a lot in the media lately about how sleep-deprived our culture is. It reminded me of my graduate school days, when the sleep study center tried to entice coeds to be "subjects." I never participated, but I was somewhat amused by the stories friends would bring back. Electrodes all over your head and torso, continual video monitoring, and sudden interruptions during the deepest sleep cycles to complete tests and answer questions . . . not my idea of fun.

The research continues to point at how the lack of rest impairs your judgment and your reflexes, resembling many of the characteristics of someone who has had too much to drink.[7] The research also strongly suggests that lack of sleep impacts your health significantly; the effects range from diabetes, hypertension and depression to cardiovascular problems.

It doesn't take a scientific breakthrough to figure this out. I mean, just wake me up too early from a nap, and you are likely to get more than your share of grumpiness and irritability. A couple of late nights, or a string of long days in the office, and I can feel my health suffering. Dr. Jekyll or Mr. Hyde? Take away my rest, and who knows who will show up?

But like restless zombies, we continue to believe culture's claim that we can work 60–70 hours a week. Mesmerized by success, we sacrifice sleep, family, health, play, naps, and self. We now live to work, instead of working at living. Stretching from one deadline to the next, merely existing to do, accomplish, and achieve, it's hard for us to fathom sacred space. To even utter it seems ludicrous.

Beyond the Sabbath that I relish each weekend, my soul needs to find ways to infuse and carry Sabbath into each of my days. The sacred space the Savior offers is a reprieve from the monstrosity of everyday wear and tear. There can be room for Sabbath in my office on Tuesday. I would do well to say Yes when Alexa and Dee ask me to come and play, even for just a few moments between phone calls.

---

7. Find out more at http://www.sleepfoundation.org.

Vacation days are there to be used, not stored. Sabbath commencing every Friday evening reminds me of the real life that Jesus has promised and the rhythm He intended since the beginning of the world. It's a gift, made for me.

"Come away with Me," Jesus is inviting, and I'm going to take Him up on His offer.

Encounter the Word

"Remember that you were slaves in Egypt and that the LORD your God brought you out of there with a mighty hand and an outstretched arm. Therefore the LORD your God has commanded you to observe the Sabbath day" (Deuteronomy 5:15, NIV).

"Then he said to them, 'The Sabbath was made for man, not man for the Sabbath'" (Mark 2:27, NIV).

Encounter

- What are you currently a "slave" to? What bondage is sapping the spirit out of you?
- Plan a minivacation for yourself today, something out of the ordinary routine. When was the last time you played just for fun (not to burn calories or compete)?
- Set up a playdate for yourself and enjoy it with loved ones.
- Set aside some time this Saturday to nap—without guilt.

6.55 Nothing

(Lynell LaMountain)

Something big is happening tonight in Poway, California: nothing.

In this town of 50,000 residents, the schools, businesses, churches, and sports leagues have all cleared their calendars so that tonight, May 22, 2006, people will be free to do whatever they want.

Kids won't have homework; there'll be no Little League games, no religious meetings, and no civic meetings—nothing. Nada. Zip. Zero. Just an evening of free time from 5:00 to 9:00 P.M. for people to practice the fine art of doing nothing.

It's not a new idea. Poway is following the example set by Ridgewood, New

Jersey, which for the previous five years did the same thing, calling it Ready, Set, Relax! I think it's a great idea that more cities around the world should start practicing.

Someone needs to jam on the brakes of this runaway train called life that we're on, speeding along so fast that our lives feel out of control and our hair is on fire as we scream from one place to the next.

Think about it. "Family comes first" is something we stopped practicing a long time ago, and it has become a faded memory of a more peaceful time. Dinner used to be sacred time for the family, but who's got the time anymore? Parents give their children everything, only to be pushed further and further away.

Ready, Set, Relax! is a concept that goes back even further than the events in Ridgewood or Poway. One of my favorite promises that I share often in these devotions is a paraphrase of Psalm 46:10, which says, "Relax and know that I am God."

To relax . . . to be still . . . to rest . . . to power down, unplug, and shut off.

Rest is so important to our health that GOD sets aside more than an evening once a year. He sets aside a whole day for us every week.

Let's do the math: 24 hours x 52 weeks = 1,248 hours of rest per year.

If you feel frayed, frazzled, and fizzled, maybe it's because you're a little behind on your rest. Turn off the phone, fax, beeper, pager, cell phone, e-mail, computer, mp3 player, television, and radio, and unwind. Get yourself a frosty glass of lemonade, grab a lawn chair, sit down, and watch the clouds float by—even if it's only for a few minutes.

Promise yourself this week that you'll set aside time to practice the fine art of doing nothing.

"Relax and know that I am GOD."

Encounter the Word

"By the seventh day God had finished the work he had been doing; so on the seventh day he rested from all his work. And God blessed the seventh day and made it holy, because on it he rested from all the work of creating that he had done" (Genesis 2:2, NIV).

"Also I gave them my Sabbaths as a sign between us, so they would know that

I the LORD made them holy" (Ezekiel 20:11–13, NIV).

Encounter

- When was the last time you had some time to do nothing? Was the time unsettling, awkward? Explain.
- For you personally, what is the connection between relaxing and knowing GOD?
- Where are the spaces in your life when you are encouraged to relax?

6.6 A Strange, Mysterious Rest

(A. Allan Martin)

Just around the corner from Maundy Thursday[8] is Good Friday.[9] Wikipedia points these out as good surnames to important holy days.

So what is the name of Saturday?

With a little Wiki digging I found it to be celebrated as "Holy Saturday," "Black Saturday" (hmm made me think of a rock group from another era), "Low Saturday," or "White Saturday."

The title I liked best was "The Great Sabbath." In Eastern Orthodoxy, it is the holiday commemorating the day Christ "rested" in the tomb of death.[10]

What a strange "day of rest." The rushing about by the Jewish crowds and religious leaders to get ready after the protracted Crucifixion. Breaking legs to hurry the death of criminals. Puncturing the side of a dead Man to ensure that all would "rest in peace." The scurry of frantic followers to bury an assassinated Icon before the setting of the sun.

*Son*down had come.

He uttered, "It is finished!" Scattered, disillusioned disciples would have certainly concurred. The grand vision of a revolution was washed up, finished, shattered, as the Miracle Man was executed.

What a strange, mysterious calm must have fallen over earth and heaven. As the torture of the Creator of the universe was coming to an end, a collective gasp of nature and extraterrestrials created gale-force winds and black holes—all

---

8. http://en.wikipedia.org/wiki/Maundy_Thursday

9. http://en.wikipedia.org/wiki/Good_Friday

10. http://en.wikipedia.org/wiki/Holy_Saturday

creation completely astonished at human depravity and Divine degradation. But now it was done, and the quiet reverence of this unholy act stilled the landscape, the space-scape. The Way, The Truth, and The Life was gone.

Light had given way to darkness. *Son*set had come.

As Sabbath morning arrives, folks are off to church as usual. Services are held, observances remain unaltered. People go about their religious way. Business as usual. The LORD of the Sabbath had been neutralized. Now things could get back to normal.

But for some, nothing will ever be the same. The paranoia was high, the shock was setting in. There was an emotional cocktail of terror, shame, and bewilderment. Once extraordinary fishers of men, their superhuman powers stripped at the very apex of what was to be the crowning of a new regime. Powers to heal—gone. Ability to cast out demons—demolished to the point of inability to cast out their own. Huddled in the crevices of the city, the followers of the Rabbi come into the Great Sabbath, heavy laden, restless.

All the while, along the streets of the city, the worship and rituals of Sabbath continue as scheduled. The bustle of temple practices, the observance of travel limits, the carefulness to observe the Sabbath doesn't lose step. Restlessness abounds.

Only One rests. In the darkness of a cave, One tastes the eternal, dreamless slumber. What a strange, mysterious rest.

Rest well, Beloved One.

Rest well.

*Son*rise is just around the corner.

Encounter the Word

"Those who walk uprightly enter into peace; they find rest as they lie in death" (Isaiah 57:2, NIV).

Encounter

+ During Sabbath time, meditate on the events leading up to Jesus' crucifixion and resurrection. What do you imagine were the thoughts of the spectators, religious leaders, and disciples, as Jesus perished?
+ Where in your life are you experiencing restlessness? What role might Jesus play in providing you with relief and rest?

6.7 Apprentice

(A. Allan Martin)

I'll admit it . . . I'm a reality TV junkie. Whether it is braving the wild on some remote, untamed island, or surviving the sharks of the corporate world, I'm fascinated by human nature and a captivated voyeur as Mark Burnett lets us peek into these fabricated "real" worlds.

But to be honest, I think they got the title to Donald Trump's show all wrong. *The Apprentice* is admittedly catchy, but it's not the reality of what the Trump "hopefuls" experience. The only times they are with "the Donald" is to get assignments, take cushy rewards, or to get fired in the boardroom. Even Trump's sidekicks, George and Carolyn, do little more than observe the apprentices and comment on their miscues. Most of the time, the contestants are left to figure stuff out while competing with "team members" who are poised to backstab their way to the "dream job."

OK, second confession . . . I'm a summer movie fan. If there are martial arts involved, all the better. Do you remember the original *Karate Kid* movie? The kid basically lives at the teacher's place, learning, listening, watching, and working with the karate guru. I love the part when the teacher is having this kid do all kinds of things that didn't seem to have to do with learning martial arts—cleaning floors, waxing the car. But in the end, these repetitious activities honed muscles and reflexes that sharpened the karate kid's skills. More than just karate skills, the student built a long-lasting bond with the teacher. The apprentice and the teacher became friends for life.

Matthew 11:29–30 shares Jesus' heart to apprentice me in a way of life that is grace-filled. As I keep company with Him, there is a freedom of spirit and lightness of being that I begin to experience as I walk, work, and learn . . . from Him. It's not a "job interview" or a contest to see if I can "outwit, outplay, outlast" others. It's about receiving from Him the ways of life He intended from before there was time: life in rhythm with the Creator—easy, light, and perfect.

The reality is that I'm glad Jesus isn't putting me on a show to interview me. I'm glad He is not looking for reasons to fire me. Everything I sense and read and learn about Jesus says He's right here, coveting time to walk with me and teach me how to live the "real" life. Although at times, I don't completely understand, He assures me that keeping company with Him will bring a good life of grace and freedom and lightness.

Teach me Jesus . . ."Wax on. Wax off."

Encounter the Word

"Take my yoke upon you and learn from me, for I am gentle and humble in heart, and you will find rest for your souls" (Matthew 11:29, NIV).

Encounter

- If you haven't seen it yet, rent *The Karate Kid*. What characteristics do you see in Mr. Miyagi that you would want in a teacher? What seemed confusing?
- How does the reality of your life parallel the struggle between Mr. Miyagi and his apprentice?
- What might you learn if you were to be an apprentice of Jesus?

6.8 Sleepin' Like a Baby

(Annette Alphonso)

Rest. What do you imagine when you think of rest? Some may see the comforts of their bed and the chance to sleep without being jarred awake by an alarm clock. Some may imagine lounging on white sand, a gentle breeze, blue ocean waters and catnapping as often as one would like. Others may imagine resting their head on a loved one's shoulder while watching a sunset disappear behind the mountains. What do you imagine that encapsulates rest?

I can't help but think of a baby, cradled in the arms of her father. Her little head is resting on his shoulder. Her body is completely relaxed and held securely in his strong, loving arms. Her face has no tension, no stress or worry. Noise may surround her, but she continues to rest. She is not affected. She is not alarmed. The security she feels while resting in her father's arms exceeds whatever exterior noise or mayhem may exist "out there." She is safe. She is loved. She rests.

In Matthew 11:28, we hear Jesus say, "Come to me, all you who are weary and burdened, and I will give you rest." Are we weary today? Are there burdens that press down on our shoulders, slumping our stature? Are we overwhelmed, overworked, and "over it"? Are we aching for relief from the rat race of our lives?

Are our eyes burning from a lack of rest and our heart crying for peace? We needn't ache or slump any longer. Jesus promised to all who are weary and burdened to come to Him and He will give us rest.

Jesus does not put a condition on the rest. He didn't offer it in exchange for something. There are no time limits on this rest. He just says come. If you are weary and burdened, I will give you rest.

Picture again that small baby, resting confidently and fully in the strength of her father's loving arms. If we can picture an earthly father, providing that kind of rest for his little baby girl, how much more rest can we find in the strong, loving arms of our heavenly Father? How much more does He, who knew us before we existed, long to rock us slowly to sleep? To kiss our foreheads as we succumb to true rest—to hold us securely as we finally have our burdens lifted and receive His love and peace.

We can find rest. We do not have to continue living burned-out and strung-out lives. If we but come to Him, He will give us rest. It's even better than sleepin' like a baby.

Encounter the Word

After reading chapter 23 of Psalms, give special attention and meditation to the following passage:

"The LORD replied, 'My Presence will go with you, and I will give you rest' " (Exodus 33:14, NIV).

Encounter

+ When's the last time you slept like a baby? What afforded you such rest?
+ What is preventing you from experiencing the rest GOD promises you? How can you experience His rest today?

6.9 Cozy, Safe, and Secure

(Lynell LaMountain)

Do you remember a time in your life when you felt cozy, safe, and secure? Do you sometimes wish for things to be that way again?

As we grow older and become increasingly more responsible for our lives, life can become raw, a little scary, and cold too. We yearn for a place where we can

relax in peace, away from the struggles and stresses of life—of survival. Don't we?

Well, while reading Psalm 91 the other day in my private spiritual focusing time, I came across some verses in which GOD promises to keep us cozy, safe, and secure. Interested? Then here they are.

"He who dwells in the shelter of the Most High will rest in the shadow of the Almighty. I will say of the LORD, 'He is my refuge and my fortress, my God, in whom I trust' " (verses 1, 2, NIV).

There's our promised rest and peace . . .

"He will cover you with his feathers, and under his wings you will find refuge; his faithfulness will be your shield and rampart" (verse 4).

There's our promised coziness . . .

"A thousand may fall at your side, ten thousand at your right hand, but it will not come near you . . . if you make the Most High your dwelling—even the LORD, who is my refuge—then no harm will befall you, no disaster will come near your tent. For he will command his angels concerning you, to guard you in all your ways" (verses 7–11).

That's our promised safety and security.

As we daily experience the presence and power of GOD within our lives, changes begin happening, and one of them is a change in our approach to life. Where once we struggled, were insecure and afraid, we're now cozy, safe, secure, and resting in GOD. Since we trust Him to know what's best for us, our souls relax in Him. It's a sublime experience.

Psalm 91 concludes with this insightful summary:

"Because he loves me," says the LORD, "I will rescue him; I will protect him, for he acknowledges my name. He will call upon me, and I will answer him; I will be with him in trouble, I will deliver him and honor him. With long life will I satisfy him and show him my salvation" (verses 14–16).

Can you imagine being satisfied in each area of your life? Wow.

This is one of the most powerful chapters in the Bible. I invite you to do what I did and print it out to carry with you so you can begin memorizing it like I have. As you internalize the promises in this chapter, you will carry a power within you that is unstoppable, secure, and always at peace.

Encounter the Word

After reading all of chapter 91 of Psalms, give special attention and meditation to the following passage:

"He who dwells in the shelter of the Most High will rest in the shadow of the Almighty" (Psalm 91:1, NIV).

Encounter

+ Currently, what is making you feel the most insecure?
+ What portions of your life feel unsafe? Unsatisfactory? How badly do you wish you could relax and feel that resting in GOD was more than religious fantasy? Explain.
+ How can you begin to be sheltered by GOD? What steps will afford you rest, peace, and security in Jesus?

My Experience

_____

_____

_____

_____

_____

_____

_____

_____

_____

_____

_____

_____

7.0 **MORPHING**

7.1 Morph into His Likeness

It is our desire to experience the presence of the Living GOD in all that we are, in all that we do, and in all that we say. We're learning to live a life of integrity like the one our LORD and Savior Jesus did—becoming apprentices of the Master Teacher. GOD is changing us from the inside out.

7.2 Single in the City[1]

(Shayna Bailey)

"Ooh, where are we going tonight?"

My roommate, Sessa, popped her head into my open bedroom door. With curling iron in hand, I was standing in front of a mirror with this month's issue of *Glamour* flipped open. I glanced down at the picture of Mischa Barton, whose hair I was attempting to replicate, before answering.

"I'm heading to Centerstage to see a play," I said, smiling. Centerstage is a theater in downtown Baltimore.

"Really? With whom?" Sessa prodded.

I could tell by her tone that she was intrigued. She had been pushing me to go out with people other than platonic friends and family for a while. Unfortunately, I was about to disappoint her.

---

1. Date of original entry: November 3, 2006.

"No one," I answered. "I'm taking myself out actually."

Sessa's expression changed to a mix of displeasure and shock. She knows that I'm a go-getter, but, come on. A date? On a Saturday night? *Alone?* I knew this was going to require explanation.

Since David and I broke up two months ago, a lot of things have required explanation. While Sessa urged me to get out there and meet new people, I refused to waver about my decision not to. When my coworkers at the hospital where I work insisted that I needed a drink because that's what broken-up, distraught people do, I politely declined. And now, even though Sessa knew that there were interested people who could have accompanied me that night, here I was heading out alone.

"It's my breathing period," I reminded her as I pulled on a pair of black knee high boots. "No dating for six months to a year."

Sessa rolled her eyes at me.

With her still lingering, I grabbed my coat and slid a champagne-colored scarf around my neck. I knew that Sessa didn't want to hear anything more about healing and GOD's will and preparing my heart. So I stayed silent. While I did a last-minute check for keys, cell phone, and cash, Sessa offered her last piece of advice for the night.

"Find yourself a boy tonight!"

It was late when the show let out—around 11:15 P.M. For a regular Saturday night, though, it would hardly be bedtime. I was tired and cold, but I rationalized that a real date would never end this way. There's always coffee, dessert, or a walk afterwards. Why should tonight be any different?

I headed to Ixia, a trendy restaurant about five minutes from my apartment. Ironically, it was postdinner *and* postwalk when I had made my last visit here more than a year earlier. It had been a good date then and a good memory. I slid onto a barstool and ordered a cup of black tea.

"You don't drink?" the bartender asked.

"Nope," I answered. I smiled, hoping that it would absolve me from further explanation. When the unique clear teapot arrived with snazzy accoutrements liquid sugar and cream in a small white pitcher, I couldn't help but attract the attention of the woman sitting next to me, though. While her date chatted with a jazz musician nearby, she took the opportunity to question me about the situation.

"You know, I wish I could be more like you," she finally said. "My girlfriends and I are always saying that we should be more adventurous. Like you."

It was a touching moment, so I decided it was probably better not to elaborate on how hard it actually is to be . . . errr . . . "adventurous." Truth be told, I had really wanted to call someone to come out with me. Like that coworker at the hospital who e-mailed me after our training session. Or, the Hopkins guy who I reconnected with at an alumni event last month. Even that annoying admirer from church who always calls "just to say Hi." All of their names had run through my mind earlier in the evening.

Ultimately, though, there is a reason for taking breathing periods. Without them, we drag our issues from old relationships into our new ones. We don't think about how we've changed and who we really are. We don't plan how to do better next time.

More than that, breathing periods give us time to consult with GOD, to find out what He would want for us. Of all the important things we're supposed to be careful with, Proverbs 4:23 (NIV) says, "Above all else, guard your heart, for it is the wellspring of life."

I am still vacillating between joy, pain, anger, regret, and thankfulness when I think about my relationship with David. It would be unfair for me dump this roller coaster of emotions into a new person's lap. Or worse, to wrap that person up in the maelstrom by expecting him to distract me from my feelings.

Besides all of this, though, I liked David as a person in addition to loving him as a boyfriend. For this reason alone, he (and every other person I've ever dated) deserves my respect even now that the relationship has ended. I mean, how else can you achieve healing and resolution if you don't take the time to grieve something that was, at some point, really good? We all deserve to remember the good along with the bad.

It will still be a while before I'm dating again, so unfortunately, I won't be writing about exotic dates with interesting people anytime soon. Until then, I know Someone pretty amazing whom I can occupy my time with.

Encounter the Word

"Now the LORD is the Spirit, and where the Spirit of the LORD is, there is freedom. And we, who with unveiled faces all reflect the LORD's glory, are being transformed into his likeness with ever-increasing glory, which comes from the LORD, who is the Spirit" (2 Corinthians 3:17, 18, NIV).

Encounter

+ What is GOD doing to prepare your heart for Him?
+ What distractions, even good ones, have shielded you from a completely authentic relationship with Christ?
+ Free to experience the adventure of encountering GOD, where would you like for your relationship with Him to deepen?

7.25 What Needs Fixing

(Lynell LaMountain)

What do you believe defines you as a person?

Is it your decisions?

Your thoughts?

Your actions?

Your history?

What?

Truth is, it's probably a combination of all those things.

But one of the defining characteristics of what it means to be human is this: *change.*

Have you ever heard someone say, "That's the kind of person I am"?

Well, that's only true if that's the kind of person they choose to remain.

Where did we get this idea that we are "set in our ways"?

Why do we have to be set in our ways? Why do we have to be "just that way," or say "it's just my nature"?

Who says it has to be that way?

When I was a kid, I fell out of a grocery cart and broke my collarbone. Sources close to the event tell me that I told everyone I met, "I broke my neck, I broke my neck!" I didn't break my neck. But what if my parents had said, "He's got a broken collarbone. That's who he is—just another kid with a broken collarbone. There's

nothing we can do about it. Good luck with that"?

Instead, they took me to the doctor and had my collarbone fixed.

Why is it that we invest time, energy, and money to fix our bodies but not our hearts?

"Oh, that's just the kind of person I am."

Baloney.

That's not who you are. As a child of the Living GOD you can be whatever kind of person you want to be. The desires of your heart are only limited by your imagination. Isaiah 64:8 (NIV) says, "Yet, O Lord, you are our Father. We are the clay, you are the potter; we are all the work of your hand."

What defines you? That's a question only you can answer.

But for me, what defines me is my cooperation in letting GOD mold me into my true self.

Encounter the Word

"So I went down to the potter's house, and I saw him working at the wheel. But the pot he was shaping from the clay was marred in his hands; so the potter formed it into another pot, shaping it as seemed best to him" (Jeremiah 18:3, 4, NIV).

Encounter

- What have you allowed to define you?
- In what aspects of your life would you like to see change?
- What might it take for GOD to shape you into what He intends?

7.3 Worriless Living

(Lynell LaMountain)

What's worrying you today? Anything?

Is anything piling on your spirit or squeezing your stomach?

Worry makes us feel as if a belt has been buckled around our chest and is being cinched tighter and tighter. It's difficult to manage the mounting pressure. All we want is relief—mental, emotional, and physical.

Stress and worry don't care, and their work leaves red welts on our soul, sometimes scars, because they are hateful, whip-wielding taskmasters.

But you're not a slave . . . you're not an insignificant nobody . . . you are a child of GOD.

It's true. And He is working in your situation *with* you.

It's easy to become discouraged when you don't see GOD doing anything for you. But here's the secret: GOD can only do for you what He can do through you.

One of the very first things we need to look for is a solution to our situation. GOD provides the solution and the power to act on it, but we have to act on it.

Grace empowers us to go and to grow.

Movement, forward motion, one step—it's our responsibility to break the inertia of inactivity, to respond to the outside force that's working inwardly within our heart.

How?

First, stop focusing on the effects of your situation and focus instead on the Source of strength—GOD. Then, second, take one step, then another and then another . . .

Don't worry needlessly. GOD is present in all your situations. And He is working in you and through you and *with* you for the best solution. Jeremiah 32:17 (NIV) says, "Ah, Sovereign Lord, you have made the heavens and the earth by your great power and outstretched arm. Nothing is too hard for you."

Encounter the Word

Read Psalm 18, and then give special attention and meditation to the following passage:

"It is God who arms me with strength and makes my way perfect" (Psalm 18:32, NIV).

Encounter

+ What impact is worry having on your momentum? What changes seem impossible?
+ What is the consequence of giving too much attention to your circumstances and the challenges you face?
+ After turning your focus toward Christ, what's the first step you feel prompted to take to enact change?

7.4 Childish

(Shayna Bailey)

"I told him that if he really believed that I never loved him, then his only mistake was not ending our relationship sooner."

Sessa raised her eyebrows in surprise.

"That's too harsh, right? I shouldn't say that."

I shifted my bare feet on the cold kitchen linoleum beneath me. Sessa was unloading Super Bowl party dishes from an insulated travel bag into the sink.

"Dude, he's acting like a jerk!" she shrieked. "You should say that and more!"

I had started regaling Sessa with the contents of David's not-so-complimentary e-mail the moment she walked in the door. Before she could remove her coat or scarf, I was flailing around her in my knee-length flannel nightgown shouting phrases like, "Guess what else?" "And then he said . . ." "I mean, does he have no memory of the past year at all?"

"Why is this coming up five months after you broke up?" Sessa asked. "What happened to make him care now?"

"He says he read my blog."

Sessa rolled her eyes. I knew she thought this was an insufficient reason for his behavior. She knew about our relationship fairly intimately—with David either at her brother's house or, later, in our apartment—and she was livid about his false accusations.

Truth be told, I was too.

I had composed a ferocious response within minutes of reading the e-mail. In between screaming out loud to no one in particular and wiping an occasional hot tear that strayed from my eye, I was violently pounding on the keyboard in front of me. When I finished the e-mail draft, I wrote and posted a blog about it just to make sure that the rest of the world was on my side too.

If David wanted to initiate a war of words, I was ready. I am, after all, a *writer*. I could devastate his emotions and his ego in a way that would make him bleed and beg for mercy, and rue the day he dared to tarnish the inbox of my Gmail account.

"I didn't send the e-mail yet," I continued. "I think I should wait until at least the morning. I was pretty angry when I wrote it."

"That's exactly why you should send it!" she said, egging me on. "After what he said to you, he deserves it!"

I wanted to believe her, but I knew she was wrong.

Time and experience have unfortunately taught me that hastily sending angry e-mails never ends well. In fact, two years earlier, one such e-mail got sent accidentally while still in composition, and the results were horrible. From that moment on, I started deleting the recipient's address while drafting, and waiting at least forty-eight hours more to hit "Send." (SK, if you're reading, I don't know if you got my apology letter, but I'm sorry that exchange of words ever happened.)

I also embraced the inherent brilliance of patience and . . . err . . . silence during conflicts—something I definitely have not been prone to during my short life. My mother still tells the story about when I was a toddler and got angry at my sister. She, being two years older, climbed to the top of my father's brown leather recliner and stationed herself there—out of the reach of my small, but probably effective, blows. When my mother finally came to intervene, she found me beating up the chair and cursing my sister out in gibberish.

First Corinthians 13:11 (NIV) says, "When I was a child, I talked like a child. I thought like a child, I reasoned like a child. When I became a man, I put childish ways behind me." More often than not, I want people to feel my pain. I will invite them to share in my joy and excitement, but when it comes to being wronged, I want my opponent to understand the magnitude of my hurt. I want to beat up the chair and curse them out in gibberish.

So, even though I wrote an immediate, emotionally charged e-mail response, sending it would accomplish little beyond providing an outlet to my anger. And let's face it, that's what my roommate is for. Later that evening, she helped me formulate brilliant, but not even remotely feasible, plans for revenge.

"Sugar in his gas tank."

"Ben-Gay in his boxer shorts."

"Super Glue. I told you how to use the Super Glue, right?"

When David and I broke up, the changes that occurred in my life were marked. I had to take some giant leaps of faith, but in the process, my security and sense of self transferred from another human being to God. I was challenged to fully embrace biblical truth in a way that I never felt the need for as David's better half.

When I finally did it, though, everything seemed clearer. Easier. Not only did I start finding answers for my questions, but solutions for my problems starting popping into my life. I started to think about the world in a different way. I began to realize the capabilities I had, that came to me only because I was walking with GOD. I was calmer, nicer, and more relaxed. I grew up spiritually.

So, it's not that I'm not mad at David. I am. I'm seething and angry and hurt. But my response isn't centered on it. After all, he'll have no idea that a change has even happened to me unless I tell him. If I don't, I'll just be hoarding the best secret I've ever found. And let's face it, that's just downright childish.

Encounter the Word

After reading chapter 13 of 1 Corinthians, give special attention and meditation to the following passage:

"When I was a child, I talked like a child, I thought like a child, I reasoned like a child. When I became a man, I put childish ways behind me" (1 Corinthians 13:11, NIV).

Encounter

+ How do you deal with situations differently now compared to your childhood?
+ What lessons have you learned along the way? What has GOD taught you?
+ With your security and sense of self based on GOD, what difference does it make when dealing with difficult situations? With difficult people?

7.45 I Think You'll Understand

(Lynell LaMountain)

My wife gave me a quote a few years ago that I read from time to time. It goes like this: "We the willing, led by the unknowing, are doing the impossible for the ungrateful. We have done so much for so long, with so little, we are now qualified to do anything with nothing."

Ever felt like that? I think we all have.

How can we cope effectively with feelings of frustration and meaninglessness?

Here are four coping attitudes that help me. Maybe they can help you too.

Attitude 1: I'm serving Jesus in them

"I tell you the truth, whatever you did for one of the least of these brothers of mine, you did for me" (Matthew 25:40, NIV).

Attitude 2: I've been called to do my best, period

"Work hard and cheerfully at whatever you do, as though you were working for the LORD rather than for people" (Colossians 3:23, CEV).

Attitude 3: I commit my work and my agenda to GOD

"With all your heart you must trust the LORD and not your own judgment. Always let him lead you, and he will clear the road for you to follow" (Proverbs 3:5, 6, NIV).

Attitude 4: Remember why

Personally, I need a good reason for why I'm investing my time, energy, and money into something. The *why* always comes before *what*, for me at least. Remembering *why* keeps you on track and protects you from the quicksand of unnecessary details.

Winners focus on the goal (the *why*). Whiners quibble about the details.

If there's been a major shift in your life and you cannot produce a good *why* for what you are doing, then maybe you're being prepared for a significant change. This is a good thing. As it's been said many times before, you can't always choose what you go through, but you can choose how you go through it.

Encounter the Word

After reading all of chapter 3 of Philippians, give special attention and meditation to the following passage:

"I press on toward the goal to win the prize for which God has called me heavenward in Christ Jesus" (Philippians 3:14, NIV).

Encounter

+ Which of the four coping attitudes spoke especially to you and your current situation?
+ What is the *why* that you have decided to focus on?
+ How are you going to go through today's challenge? How might Jesus be well served by our interaction with others today?

7.5 Forgotten

(Lynell LaMountain)

We all have days of self-frustration where we feel like Paul who said, "What I want to do I do not do, but what I hate I do" (Romans 7:15, NIV). We wonder if we'll ever get it right! Will we ever overcome our particular weakness or habit?

Many people give up. But not Mary.

The New Testament makes reference to her several times. She was the prostitute who loved GOD and, more important, whom GOD loved. Jesus kept forgiving her, and she kept hanging out on street corners.

Mary reminds us that the only sin GOD can't forgive is the one we don't ask Him to forgive.

She reminds us that GOD's forgiveness is more than mere moral absolution. Because the day finally came when you could've checked every street corner between Jericho and Jerusalem, and you wouldn't have found her anywhere.

GOD meets us where we are, but He loves us too much to leave us there.

" 'I, even I, am He who blots out your transgressions for My own sake; and I will not remember your sins' " (Isaiah 43:25, NIV).

Remember, GOD's love for you isn't based on your performance, or lack thereof, it's based on His promise. If you find that you're battling frustration with yourself, remember, you have a loving heavenly Father who's waiting to welcome you, and who'll make the pain go away. Not just once, but as often as you need.

Encounter the Word

After reading Romans 7:7–25, give special attention and meditation to the following passages:

"What a wretched man I am! Who will rescue me from this body of death? Thanks be to God—through Jesus Christ our LORD!" (Romans 7:24, 25a, NIV).

"Therefore, if anyone is in Christ, he is a new creation; the old has gone, the new has come! All this is from God, who reconciled us to himself through Christ and gave us the ministry of reconciliation" (2 Corinthians 5:17, 18, NIV).

Encounter

+ Have you ever gone ahead and done something you knew you would regret? Elaborate.

- Where have you sought rescue from character weaknesses and toxic habits?
- What role can GOD's forgiveness and restoration play in setting you on GOD's direction?

7.6 How's Your Grip?

(Lynell LaMountain)

Have you ever been tempted to quit something?

Perseverance is a key component to success in any venture.

We must persevere through failure in order to seize the day.

Most people quit. But not us. Not you.

"Be of good courage, and He shall strengthen your heart, all you who hope in the LORD" (Psalm 31:24, NIV). The hope mentioned here isn't a wish or fantasy. It's a confident expectation in the GOD who has never let His people down.

Whatever you're going through today, regardless of how difficult, challenging or disappointing your situation, remember that life isn't lived from the outside in; it's lived from the inside out.

You will prevail over your circumstances because GOD gives you the courage to persevere. He strengthens your grip and gives you solid footing. You will make it. In fact, GOD is already where you're headed—He's omnipresent, He's everywhere. You're not heading into the unknown. You're headed home.

Encounter the Word

"Blessed is the man who perseveres under trial, because when he has stood the test, he will receive the crown of life that God has promised to those who love him" (James 1:12, NIV).

"Do not let your hearts be troubled. Trust in God; trust also in me. In my Father's house are many rooms; if it were not so, I would have told you. I am going there to prepare a place for you. And if I go and prepare a place for you, I will come back and take you to be with me that you also may be where I am. You know the way to the place where I am going" (John 14:1–4, NIV).

Encounter

- When you feel like you are ready to give up, where do you gather your hope?

- When you are making the right changes and it becomes difficult, what might you ask of GOD to steady you?
- What is the destination of your life? Where are you heading?

7.7 The Best Is Yet to Come

(Shayna Bailey)

I don't know anyone who likes to move. In my four years in Baltimore, though, I've mastered the art of packing and unpacking, having lived in nine different places. Yes, you read that correctly. *Nine*. I'm moving again this weekend.[2]

Most of the moves happened my junior year of college, and there were a series of traumatic events preceding each one. That year I very literally lost everything. The first boyfriend I ever loved broke up with me and I was devastated. A few months after this, I became severely ill and was hospitalized for the first time in my life. My cell phone died while in the hospital, and no one could come to be with me for two days. After I was released, I had to take my final exams without having time to study and then get on a plane, while still very weak, to fly home. Two weeks later, I was in a bad accident and my car was totaled. I spent the next four months in physical therapy, depending on rides to get to doctors. I also lost about $5,000 on a mice- and roach-infested apartment that I moved out of (but still had to pay rent on). Not surprisingly, my grades were less than spectacular while all of this was going on. In a few short months, I went from having it all to having no boyfriend, no money, no car, bad grades, and poor health.

Every time I move, I think about that time in my life. I remember feeling so lonely and helpless. *Then I think about what happened afterwards.*

I moved into a better place. I got a nicer car. I recovered from my injuries. My GPA was still high. I met another guy. I never even bounced a check. Things not only ended up OK, they got infinitely better.

After that year, I stopped clinging to the more superficial aspects of my life and realized that GOD is in control every step of the way. My life had to be ravaged, though, in order for me to be humbled enough to develop a sincere trust relationship with Him. The blessings that were given after this were all the more meaningful because of it.

---

2. Entry was blogged August 5, 2005.

Jeremiah 29:11 says, "For I know the plans I have for you . . . plans to prosper you and not to harm you, plans to give you a future and a hope" (NIV). Do you have trouble believing this when life is hitting you hard? Trust Him. The best is yet to come.

Encounter the Word

"Blessed are all who fear the LORD, who walk in his ways. You will eat the fruit of your labor; blessings and prosperity will be yours" (Psalm 128:1, 2, NIV).

Encounter

+ What do you do when nothing seems to be going well? What sustains you through difficult times? Where do you get your strength and power?
+ What are the challenges of continuing to "walk in GOD's ways," especially when the blessings are not evident?
+ As you look over your life, how have you seen GOD caring for you in your past? When have you experienced GOD's blessing?

7.8 Meaninglessness Avoided

(Lynell LaMountain)

If you want to leave this life in a blink of meaninglessness, then rely daily on your human strength and ingenuity. Our power dies with us. But GOD's power lives on.

Trusting self isn't the wisest investment decision.

Becoming a thriving person of life and relevancy (like we've been created to become) involves forging a relationship with GOD as our Senior Partner. It means allowing Him to implant His power within us. And it's *in* this power—*His* power—we place our trust. It's *upon* this power—*His* power—we rely.

We don't trust our earning power or rely upon our moral code. We rely upon GOD just as much as we rely on our lungs to fill with air to keep us alive.

GOD is life to us. Our every desire is anchored in Him, because we are one with Him.

Imagine what life would be like if GOD was your Senior Partner in all things. Imagine what it would be like if you were filled with the Omnipresent, All-knowing and All-powerful GOD? How do you imagine your life would change? Do you think you might be wiser, more effective, more successful, and enjoy a deeper sense of peace? Do you think you might be more alive if the GOD of life moved into your life and made it His personal address? Do you think you would be more loving, and more attractive (as in magnetic) spiritually?

I'll leave you with these beautiful words today as you think things over:

"Delight yourself in the LORD and he will give you the desires of your heart" (Psalm 37:4, NIV).

GOD wants to be your Senior Partner. You don't have to talk Him into it. All you have to do is claim this spiritual reality as yours by saying something such as:

"Thank You, GOD, for loving me and giving me life. I want to be one with You. And I want our partnership to begin now. I acknowledge and embrace You as the Senior Partner of my life."

Encounter the Word

After reading chapter 37 of Psalms, give special attention and meditation to the following passages:

"To God belong wisdom and power; counsel and understanding are his" (Job 12:13, NIV).

"Delight yourself in the LORD and he will give you the desires of your heart" (Psalm 37:4, NIV).

Encounter

+ Where do you place your trust and confidence?
+ What gives your life meaning? What energizes you and fills you with vitality?
+ What would it be like to have GOD be your "Senior Partner"? What changes would that include?

7.9 Reason Enough

(Shayna Bailey)

The last time I saw her was two weeks ago[3] at Penn Station. I had taken the train back from school in Washington, D.C., and as I navigated the crowds,

---

3. Entry was blogged June 16, 2007.

making my way to the exit, I spotted her. We hugged and chatted briefly on our way back to Charles Village. Before that, it had been at least five months since we talked. So I was delighted to learn that she would be at David's for dinner.

Anthony, another Hopkins PhD student, had found what he certified as a bona fide Trinidadian restaurant, so while he and David ventured into an area of Waverly deemed "unsafe" for the rest of us, Brittany, June, Melissa, and I waited at David's apartment for the men and the takeout. We were thrilled to be together again, though. It was a long overdue Johns Hopkins University (JHU) student reunion.

"So how are you liking your program?" June asked me.

"It's great, actually, aside from pure exhaustion every day. The professors are committed, and the people are incredible. If I had gotten this education the first time around, I wouldn't have to be doing this program now."

I realized immediately that I shouldn't have spoken with the flippant tone that I did. June was, after all, still a Hopkins undergraduate. She was also a premed. I hadn't meant to sound condescending or insulting by what I said. I knew I should have been more positive or encouraging about how I talked about Hopkins, so immediately I followed up with a quick, "But I know GOD always has a plan for everything. Even with everything that happened at Hopkins . . . the failures, the discouragements . . . there was a reason. There was even a reason I was so sick and had to take that year off and graduate a year late," I said.

"I know what that reason was," June answered quickly. And then, the story began. "Do you remember how I found out about the Adventist group?" she asked.

In all honestly, I couldn't. My senior year at Hopkins, when I met June, was incredibly busy. I was running the Seventh-day Adventist campus ministry that I started three years earlier, working as a Resident Assistant (RA), taking a full course load, holding down an internship at the hospital, and writing my weekly magazine column. When I look back at those days, I sometimes wonder how I managed to survive, much less graduate in four years.

"I was struggling with my faith," June started. "Attending another church and not really knowing where I was going. Then, on a whim, I decided that maybe I should try and get back to Adventism somehow. I didn't think that there would be any Adventists around, but I told a friend, and she told me to go into that little room where the RAs always were[4] and ask. I went in, and when I asked the girl there how I could find any Seventh-day Adventists, her face lit up, and she mentioned your name. She called you that night while I was in the room with her."

As June continued talking, the memories started to come back. I'm 90 percent certain that it was my friend Angela working the E-duty room that night. She did call me, and I did pass along my phone number, as well as where our meetings were. The next week, June came to her first meeting, where, she says, Pastor Russell and I were leading. I have no memory of that meeting, but it must have solidified something for June because her attendance at the campus meetings became regular, and eventually she started attending Pastor Russell's church.

"I don't know if this is a good enough reason," June told me. "But the reason you were here that extra year . . . was for me."

June's faith had taken off in such a powerful way that I hardly even remembered how we had met three years earlier. The June I know has amazing testimonies and praise reports about how GOD has blessed her. She's the chaplain of the JHU Gospel Choir. She's the one who reminds all of us what it means to have faith. Hearing her tell me how her faith was struggling until she met me—*me!*— gave me chills.

For many years, I've wrestled with trying to understand why GOD allowed so many obstacles to interfere with what seemed like a solid, staid path when I moved to Baltimore. In many ways, it seems like things could have been so much easier. I wonder why so many challenges had to arise and if they were really necessary. Sometimes, I'm ashamed to admit that I regret giving so much time and energy to the Adventist ministry. I sometimes wonder if it was worth it—if anything I do for the church is worth it.

Yet, GOD really does have a reason for everything. And it is really worth it.

I know that not only will GOD give us all the desires of our heart (Psalm 37:4) but that when we struggle, there is always a purpose. There is always an opportunity to build our character and teach us what is really important about life (Romans 5:3–5).

Becoming a physician is really, really important to me, don't get me wrong.

---

4. The emergency duty call room.

More than anything, though, I've been praying lately for GOD to let me be a blessing to someone else. What is the point of living, after all, if you're not living with a distinct and meaningful purpose to your life? Careers and success are significant, but they don't last beyond our time in this world.

For the first time in a long time, I was reminded that my time at Hopkins *was* important. There *was* a purpose to my time in Baltimore, and my energy put into seeding and growing the ministry was *not* in vain. So, as to whether being the one to help someone else find their faith is a good enough reason to have been in Baltimore, or anywhere for that matter . . . Yes, June. It's so much more than enough.

Encounter the Word

"We are therefore Christ's ambassadors, as though God were making his appeal through us. We implore you on Christ's behalf: Be reconciled to God. God made him who had no sin to be sin for us, so that in him we might become the righteousness of God" (2 Corinthians 5:20, 21, NIV).

"Not only so, but we also rejoice in our sufferings, because we know that suffering produces perseverance; perseverance, character; and character, hope. And hope does not disappoint us, because God has poured out his love into our hearts by the Holy Spirit, whom he has given us" (Romans 5:3–5, NIV).

Encounter

+ Do you believe in coincidence? Elaborate.
+ When have you benefited from the life experience of someone else? When has your life touched another?
+ What role have your hardships and life lessons played in the changes in your life? What wisdom might you pass on to another based on what you have learned?

My Experience

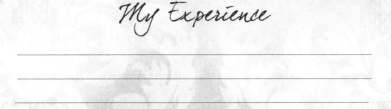

_____

_____

_____

_____

8.0 JUBILEE

8.1 Celebrate in Jubilee

It is our desire to experience the joy of the Living GOD in all that we are, in all that we do, and in all that we say. We're learning to live a life of joyous celebration because of our LORD and Savior Jesus—rejoicing and joining in His delight. We live life in the reality of GOD's victory.

8.2 Life over Death

(Todd Gable)

I've often wondered how many times in my life I should have died. I have come to the conclusion that my guardian angel will have hundreds of incredible stories to tell me. Right now in my mind, one event stands head and shoulders above the rest.

It was your normal October Sunday in Florida—warm and sunny. Like many Floridians, a group of us decided to go out boating. Wakeboarding was just beginning to be popular, and my friend David decided to embrace the sport with open arms. Not one to keep this newfound activity to himself, he was determined to include as many of his friends as he could, me included.

We got ready to go from David's house to his grandmother's on Bear Lake, where the boat was kept. I finished shooting pool with my friend Randy and climbed into the Suburban along with David, his brother Steve, and our friends Cheryl and Annie. We had one more stop to make before our afternoon of fun: boat gas.

After we filled up the gas cans at 7-Eleven, Steve pulled out onto the highway, and that's when everything began. As he was pulling out, the car in the adjacent lane sideswiped the Suburban, knocking us into the grassy median. In an effort to get us back on the road, Steve pulled hard on the wheel, but instead of going back on the pavement, the Suburban began to roll. I was knocked unconscious on the first roll; my parents and other friends filled me in on what happened next.

We rolled a total of six times. Cheryl and I and the gas were thrown into oncoming traffic. Annie was thrown out the back, and as the dust settled, she was hanging out the rear window of the Suburban. Steve was knocked unconscious but stayed in the driver's seat, while David remained both conscious and seated, although he eventually came out upside down.

Although Cheryl and I got thrown into oncoming traffic along with the gas cans, Cheryl actually landed more on the shoulder; but so did the gas, which soaked her. I was thrown onto the asphalt itself, and I landed so hard that it knocked the breath out of me, and I couldn't start breathing again. Fortunately, a nurse in oncoming traffic stopped and did rescue breathing on both Cheryl and me until we could take in air of our own accord. Another result of my hitting the pavement that hard was a hairline fracture on the back of my head. Basically I wasn't in good shape.

Later, in the hospital, I learned that that painful skull fracture—and believe me, the headaches were intense—was actually the best thing that could have happened to me. The major concussion that accompanies such severe head trauma was able to release pressure through the fracture, saving me from serious permanent brain damage. I never would have imagined that the painful fracture could be helpful.

Cheryl had a few scrapes and bruises, but was otherwise fine. Steve had to get some stitches in his leg where the dashboard collapsed onto it, and David suffered from shock for a while afterwards. Annie had it worst of all. After being flown to an Orlando hospital, she had to have her spleen removed. However, after recovering for about three weeks in the hospital, she returned to school and was able to graduate with her class that year.

There are several miracles in this story that I can see, and even more I won't find out about until I get to heaven. One is that even though Cheryl and I were thrown into oncoming traffic, neither of us was hit. Another is that there was a nurse who happened to be right there and was able to get us breathing again before any serious brain damage occurred or we suffocated to death. Then of course there's the skull fracture, which saved me from some serious debilitation for the rest of my life. Last, there's the fact that we're all still alive. All I can say is, to GOD be the glory.

As I was writing this story down, I was reminded of a passage in Psalms. In Psalm 91:11, 12, (NKJV), King David tells us, "For He shall give His angels charge over you, to keep you in all your ways. In their hands they shall bear you up, lest you dash your foot against a stone." I think that GOD definitely sent His angels to watch over us on that fateful October day, and I can only wonder how many other times they have pulled my bacon out of the fryer.

Encounter the Word

"But let all who take refuge in you be glad; let them ever sing for joy. Spread your protection over them, that those who love your name may rejoice in you. For surely, O LORD, you bless the righteous; you surround them with your favor as with a shield" (Psalm 5:11, 12, NIV).

Encounter

- ✦ What stories might your angel tell about keeping you safe or coming to your rescue?
- ✦ Where in your life have you experienced GOD's protection?
- ✦ How do you express your joy in a GOD who wants to protect and preserve you?

8.25 You Might Not Realize This

(Lynell LaMountain)

What would you do if you found $850,000?

Don Eaton, a Jacksonville resident, found an $850,000 deposit that was accidentally dropped in the drive-through lane at a Bank of America branch.

He drove home a few blocks to call police.

"At the time, I was in shock as to what I was finding," Eaton said. "I came here quickly and added it up. At that point I contacted police."

One check in the deposit bag was for $750,000. Apparently an employee of a local company was at the bank and accidentally dropped the deposit bag.

No reward is being offered.

What would you have done?

On the subject of finding a fortune, I read that a person in California won the Mega Millions lottery. How much exactly? Three hundred fifty million dollars, exactly.

Sometimes we read about finding money or winning money and we think, *I wish that was me.*

Let's change our thinking for a minute. Who owns the $850,000 deposit and the $350 million lottery winnings? GOD does. He made the world. And He owns everything.

Do you think $850,000 is a lot to Him? What about $350 million? Yes, it's a lot of money, but not to Him.

It's pocket change.

Want some good news about your financial wealth?

Consider Romans 8:17 (NIV): "Now if we are children, then we are heirs— heirs of God and co-heirs with Christ . . ."

If you are a child of GOD, then you're an heir.

Galatians 3:29 (NIV) says, "If you belong to Christ, then you are Abraham's seed, and heirs according to the promise."

What promise? The promise GOD made to Abraham in Genesis 15, where He promised to bless him spiritually and materially. In today's dollars, Abraham was a billionaire. A billion dollars is a lot of money, but it's still pocket change to GOD.

What's the point of all this? Here's the point:

You are the rich child of a loving heavenly Father. So many times we try to make GOD give us things. But profound changes start happening in our lives when we realize that He already has given us everything.

We don't have to accidentally find it, or win it by random chance, or demand it, because GOD has already offered it to us—He's offering it to you right now and is waiting for you to claim it. You are the rich child of a loving heavenly Father.

Encounter the Word

"But when the kindness and love of God our Savior appeared, he saved us, not because of righteous things we had done, but because of his mercy. He saved us through the washing of rebirth and renewal by the Holy Spirit, whom he poured out on us generously through Jesus Christ our Savior, so that, having been justified by his grace, we might become heirs having the hope of eternal life" (Titus 3:4–7, NIV).

Encounter

+ What is the largest amount of money you have ever held? What was that like?
+ How might being related to someone who was exceedingly wealthy impact you? If this someone was generous and fond of you, would your concerns and fears change?
+ As an heir of GOD, how will you now live?

8.3 Rescue 911

(Denise Badger)

Finally I was going to learn how to surf! At Pacific Beach, California, my friend Esmeralda and I took her boards down the cliff to the ocean, stopping in the sand just a few yards from the water. Surfboard, check. Wax, check. Cool surf shirt, check. We were ready to go!

After a lengthy five minutes of instruction, Esmeralda deemed me knowledge-able in the art of surfing, and off she went, confident that, with a little time and space, I would soon master the skills necessary for surfing . . . or at least survival.

After figuring out which end was right side up, and several mouthfuls of salt water later, I managed to get to where the waves were to be caught (whatever that meant). Flipping, slipping, sliding, somersaulting, and face-planting moments later, I found myself suddenly swept away on a wave! I was riding a wave . . . a real wave, and on top this time! The wind was whipping my hair back, the board was cutting the water, and the speed was accelerating by the second . . . it was incred-ible! With all fours on the board, I felt like a real pro! And then I opened my eyes, and suddenly the thrill turned to chills. First thing I realized was that there were no other surfers, and then, as I looked at my soon-to-be destination, I realized why. I was headed straight for the rocks—a group of ominous, dagger-looking, bully rocks that had a reputation for eating surfers alive if they dared come near. Panic set in as I careened helplessly toward a lot of pain. I needed to be rescued!

Ever been there? Ever needed to be rescued . . . saved from disaster, or pain, from others, or from yourself? There are so many predicaments in which we find ourselves—overwhelming temptations, family dramas, relationship issues, work struggles, school challenges . . . and we don't know what to do. We feel helpless, hopeless, trapped, in trouble with no way out. We're about to hit the rocks at tremendous speed, and we need to be rescued, now!

Enter Psalm 18 . . . enter GOD. "The Lord is . . . my deliverer . . . I call to the Lord . . . and am saved from my enemies . . . In my distress I called to the Lord; I cried to my God for help. From his temple he heard my voice . . . He reached down from on high and took hold of me; he drew me out of deep waters . . . he rescued me because he delighted in me" (NIV).

This is the kind of GOD we have on our side. When we're in trouble, GOD rescues us. It doesn't matter how many times we've done it, or how awful we are; when we call on GOD, He will respond. GOD is the one who throws us the life jacket, the lifeline, to get us out, or around, or through the temptation or struggle, through whatever situation that has us in need of help.

Psalm 18 makes it clear that, not only does He deliver us, but He rescues us from our entanglements and sets us in a "spacious place" with Him. Why? Because He delights in us! Now that is indeed a GOD most worthy of praise!

Encounter the Word

After reading chapter 18 of Psalms, give special attention and meditation to the following passage:

I love you, O Lord, my strength.
The Lord is my rock, my fortress and my deliverer;
   My God is my rock, in whom I take refuge.
   He is my shield and the horn of my salvation, my stronghold.
I call to the Lord, who is worthy of praise, and I am saved from my enemies
(Psalm 18:1–3, NIV).

Encounter

- Recall a time when GOD "saved" you in the past . . . when you were rescued, or helped through a hard time. Thank Him again for that right now . . . for being the GOD who rescues you because He delights in you.
- From what in your life do you need deliverance today? From what or whom do you need to be rescued? Picture that situation, that foe, that place of swirling water and rocks in your life, and then read Psalm 18 again.

8.35 GOD of Our Fathers

(Jeff Cinquemani)

My wife likes to go to graveyards. Not just graveyards where relatives may be buried, but any graveyard, especially the very old ones; you know, the ones that sit on the side of a hill along with those old country churches. She can walk around and read old epitaphs for hours, imagining what life must have been like for them.

For me, it's old pictures. I had the opportunity to visit the little town in Sicily where my grandma and grandpa grew up. Here, where most of my relatives still live, were hundreds of pictures, each with a story to go along with it. Unfortunately, my Italian was inadequate to ask anything but general questions. However, I couldn't help but think as we were sitting there going over all the memories and stories that I was looking into the eyes of myself, just placed in an earlier time and another part of the world.

In each of us there comes a time when we start to look back, not just on our own lives but on the lives of those who walked before us. The more we study and explore their histories, the more we find a sense of unity with them, for we start to understand the strange similarities in all of our stories.

All down through history man has had one common thread that ties him or her to generations past, present, and, yes, even future. It is the fact that GOD has and will be forever present in our lives at all times. Just as GOD was with those families during the plagues of Egypt, so He is with us today in our present-day "plagues."

In Deuteronomy 26, Moses is setting up a tradition for his people to remember the stories of their forefathers; stories of prosperity, stories of affliction, stories of failure, and stories of victory. Yet, through them all GOD was with them and brought them to this promise. It was His leading in the past that provided hope and assurance for their future. "He is the GOD of our fathers." If we trust in nothing more than that, let us move forward with the hope that He will finish what He started so long ago with those He called His own.

Today GOD is still the GOD of our fathers, and from that we can gain a unique sense of peace, knowing that He saw our bloodline before we got here. He's worked with people like us before. He's not only ready to take our lives and mold us to His character, He has been waiting for this moment for a long time, and you can bet He is excited about the possibilities.

Encounter the Word

"The living, the living—they praise you, as I am doing today; fathers tell their children about your faithfulness. The Lord will save me, and we will sing with stringed instruments all the days of our lives in the temple of the Lord" (Isaiah 38:19, 20, NIV).

Encounter

+ What about your story? Explain where GOD was in your times of pain, and in times of joy.
+ Can you trace GOD's bloodline in the generations of your family? Elaborate.
+ What are your fondest memories of GOD? Which are your most difficult?
+ What will the reunion be like for you and GOD and your family?

8.4 Heaven Visits the Hairdresser

(Sabine Vatel)

I didn't expect to meet GOD at the hairdresser's. As I sat under the hairdryer, I was reminded of how much I disliked the long waiting and sitting while the stylist ran from one client to the next. I resigned myself and pulled out a can of Pringles. Just then a small child plopped herself in the chair beside mine. She'd been wandering throughout the little beauty salon, obviously bored with the toys and books intended to occupy her while her mother got her hair done.

"Want some?" I handed her the can of Pringles.

Without hesitation, she plunged her hand in and pulled out a chip. Her eyes never left me as she chewed. She swallowed it in a hurry. I gave her the can. "You might as well have it," I told her. Without hesitation, she finished the last crumbs.

"My name is Heaven [hee-vin],"[1] she said. She put up her hand and showed me three fingers. She was in the middle of telling me her three-year-old life story when her mother came, apologizing for her daughter's verbosity. She picked Heaven up and walked to the cash register.

Heaven must have said something, because her mom paused a moment. Heaven pointed to me, twisted so her back was to me, and then swiftly turned to face me again. She kissed the palm of her hand and flung it in my direction.

Her arm was still raised in the air when her mom carried her through the door. I grinned in embarrassment as some gave me amused looks. I also grinned because I was warmed by such an extravagant gesture of gratitude when all I had spared were crumbs of chips.

When Jesus said, "I promise you that you cannot get into God's kingdom unless you accept it the way a child does" (Mark 10:14, CEV), it struck me that He was essentially speaking of our attitude toward Him. Accepting as a child does—as Heaven did—means accepting without hesitation, without shame or embarrassment for being in need. "So whenever we are in need," the apostle Paul says, "we should come bravely before the throne of our merciful God. There we will be treated with undeserved kindness, and we will find help" (Hebrews 4:16).

To accept as a child is to recognize one's personal needs and to know undoubtedly that they will be met. It's an attitude of unreserved gratitude too.

One of the more poignant pictures of GOD is of Him crying over the rejection of His people: "I have often wanted to gather your people, as a hen gathers her chicks under her wings. But you wouldn't let me" (Matthew 23:37, NIV). Could GOD be in need too—a need for a relationship with people? At the hairdresser's, I also realized that GOD is very much like young Heaven. He reaches out without any reservation. He certainly seeks for you and me; at the Cross, He extravagantly demonstrated how much He wants us.

How do you respond to extravagant love? Accept it as a child would, and—

---

1. Actual spelling unknown.

oh, why not?—pause for a moment, right now. Twist as far back as you can, then turn and throw your hands to the heavens.

Encounter the Word

"How great is the love the Father has lavished on us, that we should be called children of God! And that is what we are! The reason the world does not know us is that it did not know him" (1 John 3:1, NIV).

"The grace of our Lord was poured out on me abundantly, along with the faith and love that are in Christ Jesus. Here is a trustworthy saying that deserves full acceptance: Christ Jesus came into the world to save sinners—of whom I am the worst" (1 Timothy 1:14, 15, NIV).

Encounter

+ When and where have I experienced extravagant love?
+ What are the sacred spaces in my life where such love is permitted, endorsed, embraced?
+ Who might I share such love with today?

8.45 The Man

(Aaron Roche)

"I have been crucified with Christ, and it is no longer I that live, but Christ living in me. That life which I now live in the flesh, I live by faith in the Son of God, who loved me, and gave Himself up for me" (Galatians 2:20, NIV).

When a person decides to become a follower of Christ, they begin a journey that leads them further away from themselves and closer to the heart of Jesus. This process of taking up the cross that Christ carried can seem scary at first. The thought of selflessness and suffering for a belief isn't exactly appealing. This is why it's important to understand that Christ is living in us.

Because of this, we can endure and even rejoice in any and all challenges we face, knowing that Christ alone has already won the battle for us. This makes coming to the realization that Christ is living in and among us, the most important revelation we can experience here on earth. And because of it, we can live lives filled with joy and wonder, made possible by the knowledge that we have been made right with our Creator.

The Man I Want to Be[2]

The sun is setting sweetly on the century
and Jesus you're the man I want to be.
'Cause time can heal the scars
and send the rocketships to Mars,
but it can never show the blind man how to see.
And true my true creation may be tainted,
by people and the places that I've been,
but I've met a man who is listening
and I guess that, that's a good place to begin.
LORD please give me strength to not give in.

Encounter the Word

"But for that very reason I was shown mercy so that in me, the worst of sinners, Christ Jesus might display his unlimited patience as an example for those who would believe on him and receive eternal life. Now to the King eternal, immortal, invisible, the only God, be honor and glory for ever and ever. Amen" (1 Timothy 1:16, 17, NIV).

Encounter

+ What is the most scary aspect of becoming a GODfollower?
+ What part of your life journey has been most painful? What have you learned?
+ What truths about your life can you share with Jesus?
+ Do you believe He is listening? Explain.

8.5 Today Is Your Day

(Lynell LaMountain)

While running errands on Sunday, I saw this bumper sticker on the car ahead of me as I pulled out of Wal-Mart: *I can only please one person a day. Today isn't your day. Tomorrow isn't looking too good either.*

---

2. From Aaron's debut CD, *Already, Not Yet* (http://www.myspace.com/aaronroche).

Now, I know bumper stickers aren't necessarily designed to teach theology or profound life lessons. But after reading that slogan and chuckling to myself, four thoughts came to me:

1. Life's agenda isn't to please me (but that's what I want).

2. Nor do people wake up in the morning and write at the top of their to-do list: "Please Lynell today" (but that's what I want).

3. Being pleased isn't a lasting experience that is found in this world (but I want that too).

4. Being pleased over and over and over again is a GOD thing (that's what I really want).

Consider Psalm 23:6: "Surely goodness and mercy shall follow me all the days of my life: and I will dwell in the house of the LORD for ever" (KJV). That's the kind of pleasing life I want. I bet you do too. Pleased by His goodness, grace, and kindness every day, forever.

But is He interested in pleasing us—in giving us good things? Absolutely. Consider Job 22:21: "Now acquaint yourself with Him, and be at peace; thereby good will come to you" (NKJV). I think if GOD rewrote our bumper sticker to put on His car, it would say, *I can please everyone every day, including you. Today is your day. And tomorrow is looking pretty good too.*

Encounter the Word

"You, my God, have revealed to your servant that you will build a house for him. So your servant has found courage to pray to you. O LORD, you are God! You have promised these good things to your servant. Now you have been pleased to bless the house of your servant, that it may continue forever in your sight; for you, O LORD, have blessed it, and it will be blessed forever" (1 Chronicles 17:25–27, NIV).

Encounter

+ Where do you desire good things in your life?
+ What do you believe pleases GOD? When are you going to ask Him?
+ How do you celebrate a GOD who finds pleasure in giving you good things?

8.55 Satisfaction Guaranteed

(Lynell LaMountain)

Satisfaction. What is it?

Are there areas in your life that are less than satisfactory?

Here's the dictionary's definition of satisfaction: "The fulfillment or gratification of a desire, need, or appetite."

How satisfied are you?

There is a sentence from Psalm 103 to focus on today because of its significant ramifications: "Praise the LORD, O my soul . . . who satisfies your desires with good things" (Psalm 103:1, 5, NIV).

Wow.

As I write this and reflect on that promise, I'm remembering all the things I've done, all the things I've tried, and all the places I've searched to experience satisfaction. Satisfaction can't be borrowed or purchased. It has a single Source: a loving, heavenly Father who fulfills our desires with good things.

GOD wants you to enjoy a satisfying life. He delights in giving you spiritual and material blessings that grace your life with smiles. "So I say unto you [Jesus is speaking]: Ask and it will be given to you; seek and you will find; knock and the door will be opened to you. For everyone who asks receives; he who seeks finds; and to him who knocks, the door will be opened" (Luke 11:9, 10, NIV).

Bring your desires to GOD; tell Him which areas of your life are less than satisfactory. Claim His promise to satisfy your longings with good things, and thank Him in advance for answering your prayer.

Encounter the Word

"When we were overwhelmed by sins, you forgave our transgressions. Blessed are those you choose and bring near to live in your courts! We are filled with the good things of your house, of your holy temple" (Psalm 65:3, 4, NIV).

Encounter

+ Today in your life, what brings you the most satisfaction?
+ What are you least satisfied with? What do you desire?
+ What good things would you ask GOD to bring into your life?

8.6 Bye-Bye Blues

(Lynell LaMountain)

Do you ever feel glum, sad, disheartened, or like there's a dark cloudbank floating in your mind, blocking the rays of joy from warming your heart?

You probably do. We all do. It's a miserable mental state to be in. But, there are certain actions we can take that will dispel the gloomy clouds almost immediately. And they are,

1. Positive picturing

I believe that everything we see has an impact on us and that it affects each of us differently because each of one of us is at a different stage in our emotional, mental, and spiritual growth. The more we grow spiritually, the more sensitive we become to images, pictures, and events. Disturbing images abound.

Now, I'm not asking you to stick your head in the sand and ignore everything, because we *do* have a responsibility to make this world a better place, which means we'll confront disturbing situations, pictures, and events. But when it comes to our entertainment and news sources, we do have a choice in what we'll allow to be played in the theater of our minds. Dark, harmful, violent images, real or not, have an effect. And these images, lyrics in a song, or scenes in a book (whether it's music or books, the mind processes this information in images), can suppress and darken your spirit.

Believe me, the last thing I'm trying to do is be antientertainment. I'm a writer, and some of my friends are writers who produce films in Hollywood. I'm not an ultraconservative who's crusading for you to stick your TV in the attic or for you to never watch a movie. That's not me; that's not what I believe, and that's not how I live my life.

All I'm saying is this: if you feel disheartened, then be especially careful of what images you're allowing to be imprinted upon your mind. Because, as a result, you'll begin experiencing certain words, thoughts, and behaviors that start to show themselves in your life. If you're feeling a little "blue," then for the next few days focus on beautiful, inspiring, uplifting, positive images.

2. Walk, pray, keep walking

I'm a night person, and I enjoy being under the stars. But I usually (not always) begin my day with a short walk to "frame" my day by talking with GOD and listening with my heart for any hunches or impressions He gives me. I call it my power walk. I don't do it for exercise. I have one purpose and one purpose only, to connect with GOD.

The Bible says, "Draw nigh to God, and he will draw nigh to you" (James 4:8, KJV). *The Message* paraphrased Bible puts it like this: "Say a quiet yes to God and he'll be there in no time. Quit dabbling in sin. Purify your inner life. Quit playing the field."

In the past, I said that the Christian life isn't about right and wrong, or good and bad. And it isn't. It's about life and death.

Each day, we're "dabbling" in activities that are either life enriching and soul nurturing or life depleting and soul weakening. It's up to us to exercise our power of choice to say "Yes" to GOD—to draw nigh to him.

He won't force us, because true love doesn't coerce or make demands.

A morning "spiritual" walk is a great way to distract your mind so that your heart can have the chance to tune in to GOD's frequency. Also, this walk is for you. It's about your personal relationship with GOD. You need a personal time of worship. I'm sure that you share yourself with others. But, you need time just for yourself.

Another way you can draw nigh to GOD is to take your Bible and start reading. Let the Holy Spirit guide you to the section that you need most today. For me, this morning, it was Romans 8–11.

3. Savoring your moment with GOD

Don't rush it. Stay in His presence; practice His presence until you feel Him blessing your heart with warmth and hope.

There isn't a prescribed length of time for your quiet time with GOD. My rule of thumb is this: it's as long or as short as it needs to be. But it needs to happen. I can't live on yesterday's time with GOD, just as I can't live on yesterday's meals.

In summary, whenever you feel gloomy, disheartened, or depressed, initiate these three actions:

1. Positive picturing
2. Walking with GOD (literally)
3. Savoring GOD.

There are many, many principles and action steps that I could write on this subject. But these three steps are fresh in my mind because I did them myself this morning. My spirits have needed a little adjustment these last couple of days, and these three action steps have made my gloomy clouds disappear.

Encounter the Word

" 'They will come and shout for joy on the heights of Zion; they will rejoice in the bounty of the Lord—the grain, the new wine and the oil, the young of the flocks and herds. They will be like a well-watered garden, and they will sorrow no more. Then maidens will dance and be glad, young men and old as well. I will turn their mourning into gladness; I will give them comfort and joy instead of sorrow. I will satisfy the priests with abundance, and my people will be filled with my bounty,' declares the Lord" (Jeremiah 31:12–14, NIV).

Encounter

+ What images have been most prominent in your mind as of late? How are they impacting your attitude and perspective?
+ What are you doing to "clear the clouds"? How's it working out?
+ Where are you finding time for yourself with God? How are you celebrating in His presence?

8.65 Supercharge

(Lynell LaMountain)

If you want to supercharge your life with unstoppable power, then start doing this: praise GOD for His manifest power and blessings in your life. Acknowledge who He is and *what* He is.

What is He?

He is love, so I am loving. He is wisdom, so I am wise. He is power, so I am powerful. He is unconquerable, so I am victorious. The list goes on and on. He is

truth, so I am truthful. He is forgiveness, so I forgive.

When you acknowledge and praise GOD, you become anchored to His abiding power and presence in your life. An acknowledgement of GOD through heartfelt praise is a disacknowledgement of evil's power in your life.

Praise neutralizes evil, rendering it weak and impotent. Your good will increase when you praise GOD. You'll be a magnet for divine blessings as GOD reinforces your life with His divine presence, power, and plenty. "But you are a chosen generation, a royal priesthood, a holy nation, His own special people, that you may proclaim the praises of Him who called you out of darkness into His marvelous light" (1 Peter 2:9, NIV).

Encounter

+ What compliments might you offer to GOD?
+ What characteristics of GOD do you wish to inherit?
+ Where in your life has GOD's light been vital to clearing the darkness?

8.7 Stardust's Voyage Home

(Lynell LaMountain)

A shuttlecock-shaped space probe named Stardust flamed toward the earth before dawn, speeding toward the ground at 29,000 miles per hour. When scientists didn't see its first parachute deploy, they were afraid their $212 million mission might go bad like the probe named Genesis did two years earlier, when it cracked open upon impact after its chutes didn't open.

But, as planned, both chutes deployed, and, after bouncing three times in soft mud, the little probe was home. It had traveled three billion miles through space, including three revolutions around the sun. It had even braved a scary trek through comet Wild 2's coma, a fuzzy, dusty halo of gas, snatching the cosmic dust with a tennis racket–sized collector mitt, and taking seventy-two pictures of the craggy comet's surface during its adventure (the probe was a part of a mission to study comets up close).

Scientists will open Stardust. Inside should be about a million comet and interstellar dust grains—smaller than the width of a human hair. Collected in 2004, they're believed to be leftovers from materials that formed the sun and planets.

"Inside this thing is our treasure," said principal mission scientist Don Brownlee of the University of Washington.

I've always been a space nut. I love visiting Cape Canaveral, Florida, and seeing moon rocks and spacesuits and gazing at the giant-sized Saturn V rocket engines (the rocket that sent Neil Armstrong to the moon was a Saturn V). I've been to the launchpad where John Glenn soared toward the heavens. And I've even toured the old mission control rooms. I love space.

Rocket launches are always exciting, but for something to *return* from space, like Stardust did, is really exciting to me. I wish I could be there when the scientists look inside it.

I know this won't happen, and it might even sound corny, but wouldn't it be cool if, after opening Stardust, they found a note inside from GOD that said, "Hey kids, I'm on my way. Be there soon." How incredibly awesome would that be!

Truth is, such a note exists, carried to us by a cosmic messenger—an angel who said, " 'Men of Galilee, why do you stand gazing up into heaven? This same Jesus who was taken up from you into heaven, will so come in like manner as you saw Him go into heaven' " (Acts 1:11, NKJV).

The last chapter of the Bible contains a message from Jesus Christ Himself, who says, " 'Surely I am coming quickly.' Amen. Even so come, LORD Jesus!" (Revelation 22:20, NIV).

Won't that be a sight to behold? I can't wait to see it! Can you?

Encounter the Word

" 'In my Father's house are many rooms; if it were not so, I would have told you. I am going there to prepare a place for you. And if I go and prepare a place for you, I will come back and take you to be with me that you also may be where I am' " (John 14:2, 3, NIV).

Encounter

- When have you experienced great anticipation for the return of a loved one? What was it like, knowing they were soon to arrive?
- How can your relationship with GOD impact your emotions about His return?

- How do you imagine GOD feels about coming back for you? What will the reunion be like?

8.8 Wherein I No Longer Try to Conceal My Hatred for Animals

(Shayna Bailey)

Sessa had already been in bed for two hours when I heard her call my name from the hallway. It was minutes until midnight.

"Are you OK?" I asked, pulling my bedroom door open.

"It's not me," she said quietly. "You heard that, right?"

I had heard the loud crash in the apartment several seconds earlier. It's rare that either one of us gets up at night, but I had assumed that in the process of getting water or tea, Sessa had simply knocked something over in the kitchen. Her bedroom door had opened a few seconds before, so I hadn't even bothered to call her name or investigate.

"That wasn't you?" I asked.

Before I could finish, there was another ominous bang. Sessa screamed.

I shrieked and then jumped to what I hoped was an obvious conclusion.

"It's a mouse! It must be caught! In the trap!"

Sessa started squealing. I thought she was trying to communicate relief, but from her facial expressions, it was clear that the prospect of having actually caught the mouse was terrifying.

"What are we going to do? I have to go into the kitchen before you tomorrow morning!" she whimpered

I wasn't keen on the idea of investigating and then possibly disposing of a mouse carcass, but I knew that one of us had to. And it wasn't going to be Sessa.

I inched down the illuminated hallway toward the kitchen, fearing Sessa's screams more than what I would actually see. I had no plan for removing a body from the apartment, but I figured I could concoct a feasible plan once I confirmed the source of the noise. The thrashing resumed when I had almost reached the kitchen. Now, I was intrigued. I was even slightly excited about what I was going to find.

Unfortunately, I flipped on the kitchen light just in time to see the mouse wriggle itself free from an overturned snap trap and dart through the dining room toward the living room. Sessa started screaming again.

"If you close your bedroom door, you'll be fine," I told her. I was willing to dispose of a body for my roommate, but I was *not* going to hunt through the dark in the living room to find a mouse that I would have no idea what to do with. "We have virtually no gaps underneath our doors," I said.

"Show me," Sessa challenged.

So, standing in the hallway between the living room and the bedrooms, I pulled my bedroom door shut to demonstrate that, indeed, it would be impossible for a mouse to penetrate the tiny aperture between the bottom of the door and the heavy carpeting underneath it.

Sessa looked unconvinced. "But what about when I have to go into the kitchen in the morning?" she continued.

"Do you want to leave the kitchen light on?" I suggested. "The mouse will probably keep hiding out wherever he is if the lights are on, though . . . that means he'll stay in the living room all night."

"OK, turn the lights off then," Sessa agreed.

"I'll call the exterminator tomorrow," I promised. "I'll demand the sticky traps instead of the snap ones."

"But you told me the mice gnaw their legs off trying to escape." Sessa looked horrified.

I remembered the conversation in which I urged humanitarian disposal methods and languished over the potential suffering of a dying mouse. But that was before I had to get out of bed, witness a mouse escaping our exterminator's best efforts, and then endure my roommate repeatedly screaming in my ear. At midnight.

Encounter the Word

After reading Isaiah 65:17–25, give special attention and meditation to the following passage:

" 'The wolf and the lamb will feed together, and the lion will eat straw like the ox, but dust will be the serpent's food. They will neither harm nor destroy on all my holy mountain,' says the LORD" (Isaiah 65:25, NIV).

Encounter

- What types of creeping/crawling things scare you? Have you ever imagined not having that fear? What would that be like?
- What would the "perfect world" be like for you? What role would suffering play in that world?
- With whom or what do you just not get along? What would it take to reconcile that relationship?

8.85 Gohan and Aochan

(Lynell LaMountain)

He's dinner and doesn't know it (no, I'm not talking about a confused member of the Donner party). I'm talking about Gohan[3] (pronounced "gone," I think), the hamster that's been sharing a cage with Aochan, a two-year-old Japanese rat snake.

Zookeepers at the Mutsugoro Okoku zoo near Tokyo served Gohan to Aochan as a tasty treat after the snake refused frozen mice. But, instead of eating him, Aochan made friends with Gohan (I think there might be a lesson here).

In fact, Aochan seems to enjoy Gohan's company so much that he allows the furry (yet tasty) hamster to crawl up onto its back to take naps.

"I've never seen anything like it," zookeeper Yamamoto said, who also admitted with a chuckle that they named the hamster "gone" as a joke before feeding it to the snake. Aochan has developed a taste for frozen rodents again and is well fed. What about Gohan's fate?

Here's Yamamoto's take on it: "I don't think there's any danger. Aochan seems to enjoy Gohan's company very much."

In our world, this is an unusual story. But in our Father's world (a physical reality that will soon be ours) this is a way of life: " 'The wolf and the lamb shall feed together, the lion shall eat straw like the ox, and dust shall be the serpent's food. They shall not hurt nor destroy in all My holy mountain,' says the LORD" (Isaiah 65:25, NKJV).

Imagine a world without predators, where every being is equal, and where

---

3. http://www.usatoday.com/tech/science/2006-01-18-snake-hamster-buddies_x.htm

everyone enjoys each other's company very much . . . a world without greed, hate, or bloodshed, where unfailing love and gentleness banish "survival of the fittest" forever.

Just imagine . . . a world where rabbits chase dogs, where a lamb licks a wolf's nose, and a child naps with a lion.

Well, you don't have to imagine it because that world is real. Nowhere in the Bible does it say that heaven is symbolic, or that it's just a parable for our deeper understanding.

One of the basic rules I learned in my biblical interpretation classes in college and in seminary, is that you don't force an interpretation upon the Bible, but rather you allow the Bible to give you its own interpretation. Sometimes this is easier to do than other times, but every time the Bible speaks of heaven, a new earth, or Jesus preparing a place for us there, it always speaks of it as a real place.

So, go ahead and dream about your new home, and know that your hope is more than a wish, and it's more than a storybook fantasy. It's real.

Encounter the Word

After reading Isaiah 11:1–9, give special attention and meditation to the following passages:

"They will neither harm nor destroy on all my holy mountain, for the earth will be full of the knowledge of the LORD as the waters cover the sea" (Isaiah 11:9, NIV).

"Then I saw a new heaven and a new earth, for the first heaven and the first earth had passed away, and there was no longer any sea. I saw the Holy City, the new Jerusalem, coming down out of heaven from God, prepared as a bride beautifully dressed for her husband. And I heard a loud voice from the throne saying, 'Now the dwelling of God is with men, and he will live with them. They will be his people, and God himself will be with them and be their God' " (Revelation 21:1–3, NIV).

Encounter

- Where in your life would you wish for there to be a "Gohan and Aochan" type of relationship?
- What might be done to foster peace and friendship where once there was a "predator" mentality?

- What role does forgiveness play in your life? What will you do to foster reconciliation in your relationships?
- How might we celebrate "a new heaven and a new earth" becoming reality in the way we live today?

8.9 The IRS Observes the Year of Jubilee

(A. Allan Martin)

It's the same feeling I get each year on April 15th.

And, no, it's not the joy of spring.

I feel poor, I feel stressed, I feel like a debtor. Which is what I am. Student loans. Mortgage payments. The ten bucks Alexa spotted me when I needed to pay something in cash. I am a debtor. This becomes especially evident when the Internal Revenue Service (IRS) and I have our annual anniversary. In my dreams, I would love for the Internal Revenue Service to observe the "year of Jubilee."

In Tony Campolo's book, *The Kingdom of God Is a Party*, he says, "All debts were to be canceled in the year of Jubilee. All land was to be returned to its original owners, and those who were in prison were to be set free. In those days, prison was primarily for debtors." (18).[4]

But as I startle from this daydream (just in time to put my properly post-marked envelopes into the mailbox), I don't foresee the IRS picking up this biblical requirement stated in Leviticus 25. Could you imagine? What joy would erupt in the streets! Granted, some CPAs would be weeping, but overall I think jubilee would go over pretty well. However, such pardon is not the case with the IRS.

In fact, even the Jews never observed the year of jubilee, except for one Rabbi. Jesus read for the hometown crowd a passage from Isaiah: "The Spirit of the Lord is on me, because he has anointed me to preach good news to the poor. He has sent me to proclaim freedom for the prisoners and recovery of sight for the blind, to release the oppressed, to proclaim the year of the Lord's favor" (Luke 4:18, NIV).

Campolo comments, "According to Isaiah 61, we are told when the Messiah comes, He will bring in the new economic order in which the poor will be delivered from all oppression and freed to live life to the fullest" (19).

---

4. T. Campolo, *The Kingdom of God Is a Party: God's Radical Plan for His Family* (Dallas, TX: Word Publishing, 1990).

As Jesus took a seat, he declared jubilee: "This day is this scripture fulfilled in your ears" (Luke 4:21, NIV).

As the clock tells me that there are only five minutes left of April 15, I say, "Preach on, Jesus! Preach on!"

Encounter the Word

After reading Luke 4:14–44, give special attention and meditation to the following passage:

"Blessed are they whose transgressions are forgiven, whose sins are covered. Blessed is the man whose sin the LORD will never count against him" (Romans 4:7, 8, NIV).

Encounter

+ As for money or favors, which of your debts would you want to have paid off completely today if it were possible? What would be your reaction?
+ The familiar chorus goes, "He paid a debt He did not owe, I owed a debt, I could not pay" As for your sins and salvation, what do you wish the Messiah of jubilee would pay off on your behalf?
+ Describe what being "freed to live life to the fullest" means to you.

8.95 Parties for Prostitutes @ 3:00 A.M.

(A. Allan Martin)

One of my favorite short films of all time is Rik Swartzwelder's *The Least of These*.[5] Rik does a masterful job of cinematically telling Tony Compolo's story about a party he threw for Agnes, a low-rent hooker who had never had a birthday celebration.

The crucial moment in the film comes not as the partygoers yell "Surprise!" or as a shocked Agnes carries the cake out of the diner. It comes when Tony is found out to be a preacher, and the incensed diner owner demands to know what kind of "church" Campolo belongs to.

"I belong to a church that throws birthday parties for whores at three thirty in the morning."

---

5. Find out more about this award-winning short film at http://www.oldfashionedpictures.com/the_least_of_these.html

The reaction of the one can be seen in the faces of all those who gathered: "No you don't. There's no church like that. If there was, I'd join it. I'd join a church like that."

After that powerful line, I always end up asking myself, "Would I join a church like that?" Would I seek it out? Where is the church that parties with prostitutes, banquets with the broken, and raves with the rejected? Or maybe the more subtle . . . where's the church that loves the lonely, the losers, and the left out?

The Least of These draws its name from a powerful passage in Matthew 25:40, "Inasmuch as you did it to the least of these My brethren, you did it unto Me" (NKJV). The LORD of the party delighted in throwing shindigs in the most unlikely places. Wherever there was a cookout, you would always find Jesus hanging out, with the most unlikely crowd. Weddings, tailgating, country fairs, and graduations, Jesus likely was in the crowd . . . the wrong crowd. The New Testament makes it repeatedly clear that "the Way, the Truth, and the Life," was also the Life of the party.

Jesus reveals that the kingdom of GOD is a party. Christ came to create a church that loves to party. He loves to surprise the unsuspecting with awesome gifts. And His church parties hard—in the hard places with the hard people who have certainly found it hard to have anything to celebrate.

May I belong to a church that throws parties for the poor in spirit—prostitutes, preachers, and politicians.

May I belong to a faith that loves to party.

May I belong to the LORD of the party.

Encounter the Word

After reading Matthew 25:31–46, give special attention and meditation to the following passage:

"Inasmuch as you did it to the least of these My brethren, you did it unto Me" (Matthew 25:40, NKJV).

Encounter

+ Growing up, who did you typically invite to your parties? What were the criteria you had in mind when thinking about whom to invite?
+ When you throw a party for someone, how are you hoping the party will

make them feel? What does it say about your relationship to that person?

- Closer to home than the prisoners and prostitutes "out there," who are the "least of these" that you know and have relationships with? Beginning with those you know, what you will do today for them in honor of the "Lord of the party"?
- What kind of church do you want to belong to? Explain.

My Experience

_____

_____

_____

_____

_____

_____

_____

_____

_____

_____

_____

_____

_____

_____

_____

_____

_____

_____

9.0 **EPILOGUE**

9.1 A 24/7 Experience of the Living GOD

Like a series of photos in an album, these passages are glimpses into our lives, where we have journeyed with GOD and each other. The moments of devotion captured here are part of a process beyond our ability to orchestrate. GOD is moving in our world, and as we follow Him in what He is doing, as we join Him in His endeavors, we experience the living GOD in many ways.

In the mundane and the miraculous, GOD is changing us (that includes you). It is the presence of GOD in every moment that is startling, maybe even intrusive. Yet in the continuous presence of GOD, we begin to discover the intricacies of His love. It becomes clear that He is the One to whom we belong. In your heart you can sense it.

"I will give them a heart to know me, that I am the LORD. They will be my people, and I will be their God, for they will return to me with all their heart" (Jeremiah 24:7, NIV). It's been our delight to share a sliver of our lives with you. With great anticipation, we are eager for the journey ahead and the GODencounters yet to be experienced. Although this collection of GODencounter experiences is finite, we urge you to "add your photos to our album." Share your GODencounters with us (info@GODencounters.org). It is always encouraging to meet fellow GODfollowers and hear the stories of your experiences with the living GOD.

9.2 GODencounters Team

As part of our preparation for a GODencounters (GE) gathering, our team members are invited to spend forty days in prayer and focus. We pray for all sorts of things: participants; young adults we've invited; theme; each other; our attitude; the programming aspects.

In addition to our prayers, all our team members are challenged to author a devotional based on our Scripture-based theme. These "devos" are then posted at www.GODencoutners.org to support those who join GODencounters before, during, and after a retreat or conference. Over the years, there have been many submissions, some of which have been included in this book to be a blessing to you.

Annette Alfonso, Lyris Bacchus-Steuber, Denise Badger, Jeff Cinquemani, Tim Goff, Erika Hueneke, Aaron and Whitni Roche, and Sabine Vatel are among the many GODencounters team members who have graciously contributed their devos to this project.

9.3 Shayna Bailey

Shayna Bailey has been the author of Unplugged, the relationship advice column for *Insight* magazine for five years. She graduated from Johns Hopkins University in 2005 with a BA in psychological and brain sciences and since then has been working in the field of child and adolescent psychology. Through her work with *Insight*, Shayna has become a sought-after speaker and adviser on Christian relationships and dating. She has also written for numerous Christian publications. In fall 2008, Shayna returned to school as a full-time medical student. In her spare time, she enjoys cooking, traveling, and spending time with family. At the time of publication, Shayna resided in Washington, D.C., and was a member of Miracle Temple Seventh-day Adventist Church.

As for GODencounters, she says: "I hadn't even heard of GODencounters until I was contacted to be a part of this devotional project. After investigating the mission and purpose of GODencounters, I was impressed with Allan's enthusiasm and commitment. It was my pleasure to join this group of young adults in passionately serving GOD. As my involvement with GODencounters grows, I look forward to working with other young adults to move powerfully to reach

others. The invitation to be a part of GODencounters arrived at a particularly disappointing time in my life and has served as a symbol of GOD's promises toward us, as well as an encouragement to live more faithfully."

9.4 Elisa Brown

Elisa Brown is an accountant by profession and a passionate Kingdom Seeker by choice. Elisa is currently living out a lifelong dream of doing foreign mission work full time. She is serving as finance director for Adventist Health International–Malawi, based at Malamulo Hospital in Malawi, Africa. Before moving to Africa in 2008, she lived in the Chicago area and she helped start Oasis, a network of young adults in Chicago-land who are passionate about worship, service, and community. She also helped with planning and volunteering for GODencounters for three years while living in Orlando, Florida. During her time there she was part of the founding leadership team for Deeper, at the Forest Lake Seventh-day Adventist Church. She received her Master of Business Administration degree from the University of Central Florida in 2006.

About GODencounters she says, "My first encounter was related to the topic of prayer, and during those ten days of truly experiencing GOD, I was dumped out of my 'box' into the world of real-life experiences available with GOD! I saw the power of prayer in my own life and since then have continued to deepen my understanding about what it means to really meet GOD and to intertwine my life with His will. This experience has given me desire to see other young adults catch a vision for what it means to truly experience GOD, and that is where my passion lies."

9.5 Jeff Gang

Jeff Gang is passionate about his adventure in the kingdom of GOD and learning to live like his Leader, Jesus. Jeff is also a husband, father, outdoor enthusiast, world traveler, and Ironman triathlete. Before joining the pastoral team at the CrossWalk Seventh-day Adventist Church in Redlands, California, three years ago, he founded Deeper, a growing young-adult ministry at the Forest Lake Seventh-day Adventist Church in Orlando, Florida, where he was a pastor for ten years. Jeff received a Master of Divinity degree from Andrews University and Doctor of Ministry from Fuller Theological Seminary.

As for GODencounters, Jeff says, "GODencounters was birthed from the conception of a desire to see young Seventh-day Adventist adults move beyond their experience with GOD as a once-a-week endeavor to a full-time adventure, and my own personal journey of discovering more about GOD's desire for me to see worship as a way of life and not a weekly ritual. My own GODencounters in recent years has [sic] taken me down paths I never imagined. One of those paths has been a deeper connection with GOD that has brought me through peaks and valleys of growth. I am grateful for all that I have discovered (and still discovering) as I learn to live a GODencountered life each day."

9.6 Lynell LaMountain

Lynell LaMountain graduated from Southern Adventist University in 1989 with a BA in religion, and then from Andrews University in 1992 with his Master of Divinity degree. Lynell and Jennifer live in Orlando, Florida. They welcomed their first child into their home in July of 2007—Garrison Chase. In his spare time, Lynell enjoys traveling, diving, watching movies, and making his son giggle.

Lynell founded Life Ignited in September 2005 as a result of a profound experience with GOD that resulted in revolutionary oneness with Him. Since then, his purpose is to ignite people with life, laughter, and love by sharing GOD's pure grace to provide whatever is lacking. To learn more about his ministry, go to www.LynellLaMountain.com.

As for GODencounters, Lynell didn't really know much about it until he was invited to teach a seminar on prayer at a GODencounters retreat a few years ago, about which he has this to say: "In the fall of 2005, I participated in my first GODencounters retreat. During that weekend, the usual round of routine was shattered as people broke through the ceiling of religious indifference to touch the face of GOD. The Holy Spirit breathed fresh fire into hearts and started changing lives. We were no longer content with hearing *about* GOD because we had now encountered Him, some for the first time, and our lives would never be the same."

9.7 Sam Leonor

Sam Leonor loves being a follower of Jesus, husband of one, and father of two. He also loves his work as pastor to the students and faculty of La Sierra Univer-

sity. He is passionate about spiritual awakening among young adults, especially college students. His ministry is marked by a call to radical faith that engages culture deeply and emphasizes justice. His other interests include making music, traveling, history, and good food.

As for GODencounters, Sam says, "GODencounters changed the way I look at young-adult gatherings. GODencounters is way more than a few good praise songs and a speaker. It is a very focused, very intense gathering that calls people to not just attend, but to participate. I have been very blessed by the emphasis on deep biblical spirituality and by the quality of the worship experiences GODencounters leaders have put together. I have come to every GODencounters longing for a connection with GOD and GOD's people and have experienced both every time."

9.8 A. Allan Martin

While church planting in Central Florida's tourism district, Allan cofounded GODencounters with Pastor Jeff Gang, wanting to spark in young adults a passion for a 24/7 experience of the living GOD. Beginning as a couple dozen young adults in a back choir room, GODencounters now hosts nearly three thousand participants at their annual summer conference with several other gatherings emerging across the country.

Involved in young-adult ministry for more than two decades, Allan currently volunteers as the young-adult ministry coordinator for the North American Division of Seventh-day Adventists.

His family is his delight.[1] Allan and his wife, Deirdre, are presenters for the From This Day Forward marriage conferences. They also founded dre.am VISION ministries (www.dreamVISIONministries.org) dedicated to empowering and equipping new generations in Christian leadership and lifestyle. Daughter Alexa is entering seventh grade at the time of publication and is an inspiration to both Deirdre and Allan.

Allan serves as associate professor of discipleship and family ministry at the Seventh-day Adventist Theological Seminary.

As for GODencounters, Allan says. "GODencounters has awakened me to a

---

1. It would be important to share my deep appreciation to my wife, Dee, and daughter Alexa, who are true GODfollowers who inspire me each day. I am grateful to be in their lives.

kingdom life filled with wonder and complexity. In pursuit of GOD, the journey has been rich with experiences of Him and other GODfollowers. Where once I was simply content with my ability to talk *about* GOD and my skill to *describe* ministry, I now find myself completely dissatisfied with the religious routines I once knew. I call it *sacred discontent*. Anything less than encountering the living GOD is, well . . . less. The psalmist captured it well when he penned, 'Better is one day in your courts than a thousand elsewhere; I would rather be a doorkeeper in the house of my God than dwell in the tents of the wicked' (Psalm 84:10, NIV). Each day with GOD involves *belonging*, and *becoming*, and *befriending*. GODencounters continues to amaze me."

9.9 Sam McKee

Sam McKee is a former newspaper reporter who now loves being a pastor. He enjoys hockey, football, snowboarding, and especially hanging out with his wife and their two children. He became a Christian at the age of eighteen through a homeless man and an energetic African-American church near Chicago. Now he loves to share the joys found in Christ with anyone who's searching for something more. Sam served as a youth pastor in Colorado after graduating from the Seminary at Andrews University. Since November 2003, he has been the senior pastor of the Sunnyvale Seventh-day Adventist Church, which serves the people of Silicon Valley. His church has a large number of young adults, many of whom work at high-tech companies like Google and Intel. Four years ago, he started an innovative small-group ministry called Adventure Groups, which calls members to take what they love and use it to build community and bring people one step closer to GOD. In four years, they've grown from twelve groups to thirty-six. These small groups include inline hockey, flag football, triathlons, crafting, golf, weight management, music jam sessions, creation/evolution, and many other spiritual discussion groups.

As for GODencounters, he says, "GODencounters 2007 came when I needed it most. I traveled to Orlando as a speaker with a shattered heart. In January, I said Goodbye to my mom, who was my spiritual inspiration and best friend. She was the one who modeled Jesus' love in the tough and tumultuous family we grew up in. So I came to GODencounters stuck in a cloud of grief. But through the inspiring worship music, through being prayed over by the GODencounters team, through the warm and energetic crowd that gathers there, I emerged from a cocoon of grief into an atmosphere of hope. I knew in my head that the Adventist hope of eternal life was real, but GODencounters moved that hope down into my heart, and I can still feel it there today."

10.0 RECOMMENDED FOR THE JOURNEY

It's our hope that this is only the beginning (or continuation) of your journey, your pursuit of a 24/7 experience of the living GOD. Based on our desire to support the deepening of your devotion to Jesus, we've asked several of our GODencounters team members* to offer their suggestions of books and other resources to enjoy along the way.

Worship

Bell, R. (Speaker). (2006). *Breathe 014* [DVD]. Grand Rapids, MI: Zondervan. (Available from Nooma, 25 Ionia SW, Suite 400, Grand Rapids, MI 49503, http://www.nooma.com.)

Blackaby, H. T., & King, C. V. (1998). *Experiencing God: How to Live the Full Adventure of Knowing and Doing the Will of God.* Nashville, TN: Broadman & Holman.

Blake, C. (2008). *Searching for a God to Love: The One You Always Wanted Is Really There.* (Updated ed.) Nampa, ID: Pacific Press.

Giglio, L. (2003). *The Air I Breathe: Worship as a Way of Life.* Colorado Springs, CO: Waterbrook Press.

Hayford, J. (2000). *Worship His Majesty: How Praising the King of Kings Will Change Your Life.* Ventura, CA: Gospel Light Publications.

Labberton, M. (2007). *The Dangerous Act of Worship: Living God's Call to Justice.* Downer's Grove, IL: InterVarsity Press.

Ortberg, N. (2008). *Looking for God: An Unexpected Journey Through Tattoos, Tofu, and Pronouns.* Carol Stream, IL: Tyndale House Publishers.

Segler, F. M. (1967). *Christian Worship: Its Theology and Practice.* Nashville, TN: Broadman Press.

Sweet, L. (2007). *The Gospel According to Starbucks: Living With a Grande Passion.* Colorado Springs, CO: WaterBrook Press.

Tozer, A. W. (2006). *Whatever Happened to Worship?: A True Call to Worship.* Camp Hill, PA: WingSpread Publishers.

Gospel

Blanchard, K. (1994). *We Are the Beloved.* Grand Rapids, MI: Zondervan.

Curtis, B. & Eldredge, J. (1997). *The Sacred Romance: Drawing Closer to the Heart of God.* Nashville, TN: Thomas Nelson.

Eldredge, J. (2004). *Epic: The Story God Is Telling and the Role That Is Yours to Play.* Nashville, TN: Thomas Nelson.

Feinberg, M. (2007). *The Organic God.* Grand Rapids, MI: Zondervan.

Ortberg, J. (2001). *If You Want to Walk on Water, You've Got to Get Out of the Boat.* Grand Rapids, MI: Zondervan.

Thomas, J. D. (2002). *Messiah: A Contemporary Adaptation of the Classic Work of Jesus' Life, "The Desire of Ages."* Nampa, ID: Pacific Press.

Venden, M. (2003). *95 Theses on Righteousness by Faith: Apologies to Martin Luther.* Nampa, ID: Pacific Press.

———. (1992). *Love God and Do as You Please: A New Look at the Old Rules.* Nampa, ID: Pacific Press.

White, E. (1892). *Steps to Christ.* Hagerstown, MD: Review and Herald.

Willard, D. (1997). *The Divine Conspiracy.* San Francisco: HarperCollins.

Grace

Claiborne, S. (2006). *The Irresistible Revolution: Living as an Ordinary Radical.* Grand Rapids, MI: Zondervan.

Daniells, A. G. (1941). *Christ Our Righteousness.* Hagerstown, MD: Review & Herald.

Miller, D. (2003). *Blue Like Jazz: Nonreligious Thoughts on Christian Spirituality.*

Nashville, TN: Thomas Nelson.

Swindoll, C. (1990). *Grace Awakening*. Dallas, TX: Word Publishing.

Volf, M. (2006). *Free of Charge: Giving and Forgiving in a Culture Stripped of Grace*. Grand Rapids, MI: Zondervan.

Yaconelli, M. (2007). *Messy Spirituality*. Grand Rapids, MI: Zondervan.

Yancey, P. (1997). *What's So Amazing About Grace?* Grand Rapids, MI: Zondervan.

Prayer

Bell, R. (Speaker). (2008). *Open 019* [DVD]. Grand Rapids, MI: Zondervan. (Available from Nooma, 25 Ionia SW, Suite 400, Grand Rapids, MI 49503, http://www.nooma.com.)

Adam, D. (1997). *The Rhythm of Life: Celtic Daily Prayer*. New York: Morehouse Publishing.

Eldredge, J. (2008). *Walking With God: Talk to Him. Hear From Him. Really.* Nashville, TN: Thomas Nelson.

Foster, R. (1992). *Prayer: Finding the Heart's True Home*. New York: HarperOne.

Greig, P. (2007). *God on Mute: Engaging the Silence of Unanswered Prayer*. Ventura, CA: Regal Books.

Greig, P., & Roberts, D. (2006). *Red Moon Rising: How 24-7 Prayer is Awakening a Generation*. Orlando, FL: Relevant Media Group.

Morris, D. (2008). *The Radical Prayer*. Hagerstown, MD: Autumn House.

Northumbria Community (2002). *Celtic Daily Prayer: Prayers and Readings From the Northumbria Community*. New York: HarperOne.

Sabbath

Buchanan, M. (2006). *The Rest of God: Restoring Your Soul by Restoring Sabbath*. Nashville, TN: Thomas Nelson.

Dawn, M. (1989). *Keeping the Sabbath Wholly: Ceasing, Resting, Embracing, Feasting*. Grand Rapids, MI: William B. Eerdman's Publishing.

Hershey, T. (Speaker). (2003). *The Art of Doing Nothing: Letting Our Souls Catch Up With Our Bodies* [DVD]. (Available from Terry Hershey, PO Box

2301, Vashon, WA 98070, http://www.terryhershey.com.)

Heschel, A. (2003). *The Sabbath: Its Meaning for Modern Man*. Boston, MA: Shambhala.

Muller, W. (1999). *Sabbath: Finding Rest, Renewal, and Delight in Our Busy Lives*. New York: Bantam.

Winner, L. (2003). *Mudhouse Sabbath*. Brewster, MA: Paraclete Press.

Morphing

Antonucci, V. (2008). *I Became a Christian and All I Got Was This Lousy T-shirt: Replacing Souvenir Religion With Authentic Spiritual Passion*. Ada, MI: Baker Publishing.

Blake, C. (2007). *Swimming Against the Current: Living for the God You Love*. Nampa, ID: Pacific Press.

Dybdahl, J. L. (2008). *Hunger: Satisfying the Longing of Your Soul*. Hagerstown, MD: Autumn House.

Foster, R. (1998). *Celebration of Discipline*. London, UK: Hodder & Stoughton Ltd.

Mulholland, M. R. (1993). *Invitation to a Journey: A Road Map for Spiritual Formation*. Downer's Grove, IL: InterVarsity Press.

Ortberg, J. (2002). *The Life You've Always Wanted: Spiritual Disciplines for Ordinary People* (Expanded ed.). Grand Rapids, MI: Zondervan.

Palmer, P. J. (1990). *The Active Life*. San Francisco, CA: Jossey-Bass Publishers.

Weatherhead, L. (1990). *The Transforming Friendship: A Book About Jesus and Ourselves*. Nashville, TN: Abingdon Press.

White, E. (2008). *The Sanctified Life*. Hagerstown, MD: Review and Herald.

———. (1892). *Steps to Christ*. Hagerstown, MD: Review and Herald.

Willard, Dallas. (1988). *The Spirit of the Disciplines: Understanding how God Changes Lives*. New York: HarperCollins.

———. (2002). *Renovation of the Heart: Putting on the Character of Christ*. Colorado Springs, CO: NavPress.

Jubilee

Campolo, T. (1990). *The Kingdom of God Is a Party: God's Radical Plan for His Family*. Dallas, TX: Word Publishing.

McManus, E. (Speaker). (2008). *Party Theology.* (Available from http://www.mosaic.org.)

Myers, C. (2001). *The Biblical Vision of Sabbath Economics.* Washington, DC: Tell the Word-Church of the Saviour.

Zander, B. & R. (2002). *The Art of Possibility: Transforming Professional and Personal Life.* New York: Penguin Press.

*GODencounters leaders recommending these titles include:

Ryan Bell *was the presenter for GODencounters 2003. He is also the senior pastor for the Hollywood Seventh-day Adventist Church.*

Elisa Brown *served as volunteer coordinator for GODencounters 2005 and has presented across the country about this young adult movement. She is also director of finance for Adventist Health International, Malawi, Africa.*

Tami Cinquemani *was part of the volunteer team for GODencounters 2002–04. She is also the pastoral assistant for Florida Hospital Seventh-day Adventist Church.*

Adam Heck *has been one of the young adult hosts for GODencounters since 2007. He is also an instructor at Florida Hospital College of Health Sciences.*

Dany Hernandez *is the coordinator for GODencounters 2008. He is also the pastor for Deeper, a young adult worship service of the Forest Lake Seventh-day Adventist Church.*

Marc Judd *was worship leader and presenter for GODencounters 2002. Along with practicing medicine, he and his wife, Andrea, are part of the contemporary Christian group, Faith First. In addition to songwriting, Marc has been leading congregations in worship for nearly two decades.*

Andy McDonald *has been part of the pastoral support team for GODencounters since 2001. He is also the senior pastor of the Florida Hospital Church of Seventh-day Adventists.*

A. Allan Martin *started GODencounters and serves as curriculum coach. He is also associate professor of Discipleship & Family Ministry at the Seventh-day Adventist Theological Seminary.*

Alex Pinilla *has been part of the pastoral support team for GODencounters since 2003. He is also senior pastor for the New Community Church of Seventh-day Adventists.*

My Experience

My Experience